BEAD
Romantique
ELEGANT BEADWEAVING DESIGNS

Lisa Kan

INTERWEAVE
interweavebooks.com

Photography
Joe Coca

Illustrations
Bonnie Brooks

Cover design
Paulette Livers

Interior design
Paulette Livers and
Pamela Norman

Technical Editor
Bonnie Brooks

Interweave Press LLC
201 East Fourth Street
Loveland, CO 80537-5655 USA
interweavebooks.com

Printed in China by Asia Pacific Offset

Library of Congress Cataloging-in-Publication Data
Kan, Lisa.
  Bead romantique : elegant beadweaving designs / Lisa Kan.
    p. cm.
  Includes bibliographical references and index.
  ISBN 978-1-59668-046-3 (pbk.)
  1. Jewelry making. 2. Beadwork. I. Title.
  TT212.K36 2008
  745.594'2--dc22
                          2007029453

10 9 8 7 6 5 4 3 2

*This book could not have
been written without the support
of my most enthusiastic fan and
husband, Nicholas Pisano—you
did everything so I could focus
on my art and writing.
I am the luckiest woman alive.*

ACKNOWLEDGMENTS

I would like to thank my parents, Shek Wan and Chau Ngor Kan, from whom I inherited my work ethic and who supplied me with much inspiration in my youth with their textile business. Thanks also go to my sisters, Sandy and Tina, for their love and support.

To Tricia Waddell, who believed in my initial concept, thank you for giving me the freedom to create my vision and providing me with this great opportunity. To Marlene Blessing, thank you for your friendship, guidance, and always challenging me with tight deadlines. This book would not have been written without the two of you! And to both my editors, Katrina Vogel and Bonnie Brooks, my heartfelt thanks for your hard work and expertise. I can't imagine completing this book without the two of you. Thanks also go to the following special people at Interweave: Linda Stark, Linda Ligon, Rebecca Campbell, Joe Coca, Laura Levaas, Paulette Livers, Jaime Guthals, Kerry Flint, and Ann Swanson.

Thank you to all my beading "teachers" for nurturing my beading through your articles, books, and workshops. Special thanks also go to Kelly Russell, Jannell Botto, Hwa Soo Park, Sun Young Park, Wendy Mullane, Jess Italia, and Jeanne Holland, for your generous donations to this book. And to Kelly Thompson, who owns and operates the San Gabriel Bead Company, where my journey as a glass and bead artist first began. You have always supported me since my humble beginnings. Thank you!

And most importantly, to my customers and "students," thank you for your encouragement, appreciation, and constantly inquiring if I would ever consider writing a book. Well here's the first one—did I keep you guessing? I hope to continue teaching through my writing, reaching more people than I would in a classroom setting.

CONTENTS

The Projects

WELCOME TO MY ROMANTIC SIDE

How often does one get an opportunity to write a book that will make a mark in the beading world, share with others their passion for beads, and be cataloged in the Library of Congress? Even before Interweave Press approached me about writing this book I had already begun writing it in my dreams. But this was not a dream, and after nearly a year of hard work (with the help of many talented folks noted in the acknowledgments) I give you this book.

Why have I chosen to give away my techniques and designs? Because by giving and sharing, one receives many intangible rewards that enrich the creative soul. Because it allows an artist to further grow and be challenged themselves. Because it provides inspiration to others who share in my passion for the creative process and opens up new possibilities. Because it allows me to pay tribute to a craft that has brought me so much pleasure.

I've always believed that if you create from your heart and design what you love, it will show in the finished work. When asked what I would write about, it was easy because my style of beadwork imbues a sense of femininity and romance. I wanted to design and create beadwork that would be wearable, beautiful and elegant, while also paying tribute to historical jewelry designs. Write about what you know, create what you love, and design with a vision.

Without history, there is no present. In such a fast-paced world with commercial goods and imports, the appreciation for handiwork is dwindling. Lacking also were beading books catering to the intermediate and advanced beader. I wanted to do my part to continue promoting the craft.

I enjoy building on the standard stitches, resulting in a design that appears complex but is created using simple techniques, therefore showing the endless possibilities of each stitch. Although the projects in this book may look complicated, never fear! All the steps have been broken down, and many of the projects are based on similar components. I hope as you flip through the pages that each design will progressively get you excited to attempt the next. I would love to hear your comments, and if you ever get stumped, feel free to send me an e-mail at *LisaKanDesigns@yahoo.com.*

MATERIALS AND TOOLS

By mixing and weaving a harmonious blend of beads in varying colors, finishes, and shapes, you can create beautiful heirloom-quality jewelry. The key to getting a good start is the selection of quality materials. Time and attention to the details will also enhance the final result of your beadwork. Be in the right mindset when you sit down to bead. Remember to take breaks often to rest your eyes, fingers, and back so your beading sessions are more productive. How well you execute a project is more important than the speed at which you complete it. Be playful and discover new ways of implementing each beading stitch. Keep your mind and options open as there are "infinite possibilities" literally at the tips of your fingers.

BEAD SELECTION

SEED BEADS come in a variety of sizes. The size is indicated by a number, the larger the numbered size (6°, 8°, 10°, 11°, 13°, 15°, etc.), the smaller the bead. The seed beads used throughout this book are mostly Japanese, in various shapes, sizes, colors, and finishes. Miyuki, Toho, and Matsuno are the three major manufacturers of Japanese seed beads. Toho beads have the largest holes amongst the three, but all Japanese seed beads have larger holes than other seed beads. Some colors cross over between the three manufacturers (albeit with different color numbering) and can be used interchangeably.

Be aware that bead shops do not have a consistent color naming or numbering methodology. I highly recommend not using any galvanized beads because the color tends to rub off if not sealed. Technology is improving to make these metalized beads colorfast, but it is still in the early stages of development.

COLOR COMBINATIONS are important in beadwork, and having a basic understanding of it will help you select color combinations. There is a series of books entitled *Color Harmony* (Rockport Publishers) that I have found indispensable for color combination ideas. Blending matte and shiny, and transparent and opaque beads can create subtle texture that reflects light. Beads like Swarovski crystals, Czech firepolished beads, semiprecious stones, freshwater pearls, or different shaped seed beads are a few options. Faceted cuts and vintage (glass, Lucite, plastic, French steel cut, etc.) beads can also bring an old-world feel to contemporary designs. I tend to use muted and subdued colors to imbue an old-world feel. I have favorite colors that I always go to and over time, you will as well. Remember that beads may change in color in the final beadwork based on nearby beads and the thread used so never depend on the color you see when looking at a tube.

VINTAGE BEADS are no longer manufactured due to the toxicity of the chemicals used to create some of the fabulous colors and finishes; therefore, they are highly coveted and can be rather expensive. This is the case for glass beads as well as vintage Swarovski crystals/rhinestones. For glass beads, some of the vintage molds are being used today with modern glass recipes. These are sold as "vintage reproductions." Sometimes you may even be lucky enough to find glass beads made with vintage molds and vintage glass. These beads are made when raw vintage glass is found leftover in a warehouse. If you do decide to use vintage beads, be sure to check for uniformity if the bead is coated with a finish and ensure that there are no chips or imperfections. Some slightly imperfect beads can still be used to add a bit of "history" to your beadwork. The adage of "you get what you pay for" is true in this instance. Do not use cheaper components especially when you are beading an elaborate design. It will definitely show.

THREAD SELECTION

Thread color is an important consideration in beadwork because it affects the final color, especially on transparent beads. Always try to select thread color to match closely to the beads you are using. I have included descriptions of my favorite threads here, but there are many types of thread available on the market (Nymo, C-Lon, Dandyline, etc.), and I encourage you to experiment and find those that work best for your beading style.

SILAMIDE is a twisted, pre-waxed nylon thread that is available in 100-yard cards and in 500-yard spools in one size (Size A). Although there is a limited selection of colors compared to other threads, I prefer it because it does not fray or tear apart when I have to backtrack to remove stitches. The Silamide light brown is a neutral color that blends well with most beadwork and is my favorite color. Furthermore you only need to condition this thread by pre-stretching before beading since it is pre-waxed. Beeswax or Thread Heaven is only used on the ends before threading. Be aware that the ends of crystals have sharp ends that will cut through Silamide over time.

POWERPRO is a very strong braided and pre-waxed thread that can also be used for beadwork with crystals. It is available in several weights and made in white or moss green. Because of different dye lots, the moss green often times ranges from light to dark.

FIRELINE is a stiff nylon fishing line that has transitioned into the beading world and is a cost-effective alternative to PowerPro. This thread comes in several strength tests and is available in crystal clear, gray, or flame green colors. It does not tangle easily, and no waxing or conditioning is required. The number of bead passes you make determines the weight used. I prefer using either 6 lb or 8 lb weights in clear when working with light-colored beads and gray for darker-colored beads. The gray FireLine has a tendency to rub off so be aware of this when your fingers start appearing "dirty." I use FireLine when I desire stiffer beadwork or for designs that incorporate crystals because it is not easily cut by their sharp edges. Flatten the ends with your fingernails or chain-nose pliers before threading.

NEEDLE SELECTION

There are many different types of beading needles; long, short, sharp, etc. But the most important aspect for the projects in this book is the needle size.

PONY BEADING NEEDLES in size 12 are often what I use in my work because they have larger eyes for easier threading and are reasonably priced compared to other needles. The Pony needles tend to be a bit more susceptible to bending with use but chain-nose pliers usually come to the rescue.

JOHN JAMES BEADING NEEDLES in size 13 are used for smaller-hole beads (such as Czech seed beads and char-lottes) and when making multiple passes. I have found this brand very dependable, and they are a good alternative if you cannot locate Pony needles.

The larger the number in needle size, the thinner the needle and the smaller the eye. Size 12 needles are nice if you have multiple passes, but if you have fewer passes and are working with larger-hole beads, you may feel more comfortable with size 10 needles. Size 13 needles can be used with smaller-hole beads. As with thread choice, I recommend that you try all kinds and use the brand of needles you prefer.

TOOLS

ROUND- AND CHAIN-NOSE PLIERS are indispensable for your tool box. I prefer Lindstrom RX pliers with the blue handle and bio-spring. These are the most comfortable pliers I have found available in the market. Made in Sweden, they are simply the best and guaranteed for life! As with beads, do not skimp on your tools!

I also use chain-nose pliers to finish 2×2mm Tornado crimp tubes. The Tornado crimp tube can simply be pressed with the chain-nose pliers to create a secure finish and an ornate spiral design. If you are trying to avoid buying yet another tool, the Tornado crimp tubes are a wonderful option for finishing off your strung projects.

Chain-nose pliers come in handy in beadwork as well, to straighten bent needles or to pull needles through a tight spot.

MAGIC CRIMPING PLIERS are very helpful when finishing strung designs. They are made to be used with only the 2×2mm crimp beads. This tool forms the tube-shaped crimp bead into a nearly round bead. This allows you to not only create a connection point but also add a design element. How ingenious! There are two available tools, one for 0.014 and another for 0.019 beading wire.

around to ensure
l look. I use
tters that are of
pinch the wire

ity (such as

rn the ends of
lighter but those
ve heard stories

BEADING PADS are very helpful for keeping track of beads and needles. I use a velvet jewelry pad that has a stiff cardboard interior wrapped in foam. This surface makes it easier to pick up beads and also provides a place to pin extra needles while I work.

AN OTTLITE or another lamp that emulates daylight (about a 5,000 Kelvin rating) is very important. Color is very important in beadweaving and you cannot see the true color of your beads if you do not have proper lighting. ➔

TIPS AND TRICKS

INSPIRATION

I am often asked where I find inspiration for my designs. The answer is "everywhere." There are ideas all around you. Don't limit yourself to the obvious but look outside of the ordinary. For instance, I find color inspiration at the yarn or fabric store, in gardening and quilt books, and even the paint-chip aisle of the local hardware store. I collect images from magazines and keep them in a binder. I also browse vintage jewelry listings on eBay, because it is fun and free.

MAKING SAMPLES

When making a large design, make a small sample first to evaluate the color harmony and balance before moving forward. More than likely if you don't like the way the sample looks, you won't like it in a larger piece. I have been known to cut up beadwork and start over. Don't fear those words "start over."

STOP OR TENSION BEADS

Although the projects do not mention the use of a stop bead, if you find it difficult to hold your beadwork when initially stringing beads you can use a stop bead to hold your beadwork in place. Use a bead that is larger, and a different color, than those in your design so that you can easily spot it later for removal. String the bead and pass through it twice more, leaving the appropriate tail length for your project. Be careful not to split the thread on the second pass so that the bead will be able to slide off easily when you are ready to remove it. Remember to take out your stop bead before continuing!

HOLDING YOUR BEADWORK

The way you hold your beadwork and the direction you bead determines the tension of your beadwork. Tension is very important, and with practice you will find a happy medium. I hold my work on my left between my thumb and forefinger, beading with my right. When I am doing a complex connection that requires thread tension, I sometimes wrap the working thread around my right forefinger several times.

THREAD LENGTHS

I use from 1 to 1.5 yd (91.5 cm to 1.4 m) of a single length of thread for most bead starts, as this is the most comfortable length to avoid knots and tangles. I rarely use double thread as I find it difficult to undo if you make an error and have to backtrack. If longer thread is required, as in a spiral rope, I use a No-Tangle Thread Bobbin to roll up half the length to avoid having to reconnect new thread too often. Some beaders prefer shorter lengths for faster beading. Use the length that is comfortable for you.

ADDING NEW THREAD

When beading an elaborate project, you will invariably run out of thread. When you have about 4 inches (10.5 cm) remaining of the working thread, with the new thread weave about 1 inch (2.5 cm) away into several beads, leaving a 2 to 3 inch (5–8 cm) tail, pass under the thread from a previous pass and make a half hitch knot. Follow the thread path of the stitch and repeat with another knot. Weave to the location of the original thread and tie a square knot. Continue beading with the new thread. Weave the old thread into the newly beaded stitches by repeating a half hitch knot through several beads later. Thread can be added in many ways as long as it does not show—it doesn't matter which method you adopt.

TURNING

In many of the beading projects, a quick way to turn the weaving direction is to pass under the thread from a previous pass and make an overhand knot. Then weave back toward the direction you want, creating a half hitch knot. Keep in mind to always follow the thread path of whatever stitch you are using so no thread shows through.

FINISHING

To finish the ends of your beadwork, different threads require different treatments. Some beaders will weave the tail thread through several beads again and again and then just trim. However, I generally make at least two to three half hitch knots between several beads at each interval before I trim. For Silamide, cut close to the beadwork and add a dab of clear nail polish to the ends to prevent frays or use a thread zapper. For FireLine, you can use flush cutters to trim (there is no need for further treatment).

BURNISHING

In metalwork, generally a hard steel burnishing tool is used to rub back and forth on metal to create a shiny polished surface and also to secure a stone or cabochon to its bezel. For our purposes, I have substituted a wooden dowel or ruler for the burnishing tool to complete bezel-setting brass filigree wraps. Be sure to burnish in one direction and add additional pressure as necessary to avoid damaging the brass findings. Burnishing will work harden the metal.

To burnish a coin pearl that has been wrapped in a brass filigree, cushion the component with your forefinger and thumb. With your dominant hand, exert pressure with the wood tool on one of the prongs toward the center, while performing an arching and curving motion following the shape of the pearl. Rotate to the opposite prong and repeat. Repeat on remaining two prongs.

To burnish a brass bead cap to a glass bead, exert pressure with the wood tool in a downward motion, following the shape of the bead while performing an arching and curving motion. Rotate and repeat on remaining three prongs.

ANTIQUING WITH LIVER OF SULFUR

Oxidizing metals chemically can be achieved through the use of liver of sulfur (a.k.a. potassium sulfide) or commercially available oxidizing solutions. Metal will also naturally oxidize over time when exposed to air and dampness. When using a sulfur solution, a thin film forms on the surface of the metal resulting in discoloration (the patina). This color is only on the surface, and over time the patina can be lost, unless sealed with lacquer or beeswax. Liver of sulfur is generally sold in canisters in rough lumps. After opening the can, tightly seal and avoid prolonged exposure to light or air, which can reduce the lifespan and effectiveness of liver of sulfur. Store the canister in a cool, dark place.

When liver of sulfur is used in a warm solution of water, silver and golds less than 18k will turn a range of colors from warm yellows, blues, pinks, and purples to gray. A few drops of household ammonia can also be added to the solution to get more intense blues. The use of baking soda will deepen browns.

Work in a well-ventilated space with access to running water. Metal that is to be oxidized needs to be completely cleaned. The solution is most effective when it is deep yellow and dissolved in warm (not boiling) water. Mix only the amount you need for one application because the solution spoils rapidly. Only a pea-size chunk to a cup of water is needed to begin, and the solution can be intensified, as desired. For a pendant such as the Nouveau bead used on p. 68, use a cotton swab or fine paintbrush to paint the solution onto the bail. When you have achieved the color you want, rinse the piece thoroughly in water because any solution left on the silver will continue to darken. →

Scalloped Chain
NECKLACE

I just love mixing chain into my designs because it adds a sense of fluidity with every movement. The simplicity in this design is balanced by the central focal bead. The scallop layout is reminiscent of the hems of flapper-style dresses of the 1920s. Every which way you swing, the necklace moves with you. And even when you are standing or sitting still, the light catches the facets on the fancy cut focal drop. This necklace would look especially beautiful with a V neckline.

MATERIALS
12x16mm faceted citrine focal drop

126 aquamarine 2x3mm to 3x4mm faceted rondelles

66 vermeil 2x2mm cornerless cubes

104" (264.5 cm) of cable chain (with 2mm links)

38mm gold-filled hook clasp

2 gold-filled 2x2mm crimps

18" (46 cm) of gold 0.014 beading wire

TOOLS
Magic Crimping Pliers

Flush cutters

Optional: Necklace stand

SIZE
17" (43.5 cm)

TECHNIQUE
Stringing, crimping

The scallop portions are divided into three sections.

SECTION 1

→1 Cut the cable chain into twelve 4" (10.5 cm) and seven 8" (20.5 cm) lengths.

→2 String a rondelle, a 4" (10.5 cm) chain, a rondelle, and a cube. Repeat this sequence five more times.

→3 String a rondelle, an 8" (20.5 cm) chain, the opposite end of the first 4" (10.5 cm) chain strung, a rondelle, and a cube. Repeat this sequence five more times, each time stringing the opposite ends of the 4" (10.5 cm) chains already strung, in the same order.

SECTION 2

→4 String a rondelle, the last 8" (20.5 cm) chain, a rondelle, and a cube.

→5 String a rondelle, a cube, and the gemstone focal bead.

→6 String a cube, a rondelle, a cube, a rondelle, and the opposite end of the 8" chain just strung.

→7 String a rondelle, a cube, a rondelle, the opposite end of the sixth 8" (20.5 cm) chain strung, and a 4" (10.5 cm) chain. Repeat this sequence five more times, each time stringing the opposite ends of the 8" (20.5 cm) chains already strung, in the reverse order.

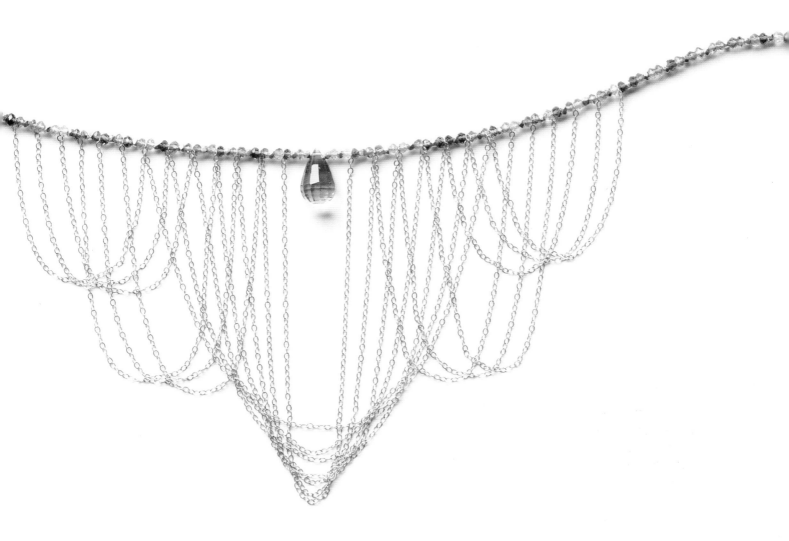

SECTION 3

→**8** The scallops, in the third section, will mirror the first section. In order to achieve this, the 4" (10.5 cm) chains strung in Section 2 must be laid in front of the 8" (20.5 cm) scallops made in Section 2.

→**9** String a rondelle, a cube, a rondelle, and the opposite end of the first 4" (10.5 cm) chain from Section 2. Repeat this sequence five more times, each time stringing the opposite ends of the 4" (10.5 cm) chains already strung, in the same order.

→**10** String a rondelle.

COMPLETING THE NECKLACE

→**11** String a cube and two rondelles. Repeat this sequence seventeen more times.

→**12** String a cube and a crimp bead.

→**13** String through one end of the clasp and then back into the crimp bead. Make sure the beading wires are parallel and crimp, according to manufacturer's instructions.

→**14** Repeat Steps 11 to 13 on the opposite side of the necklace.

Ndebele Pearl Medallion
EARRINGS AND BRACELET

While exploring how Ndebele stitch could be gradually increased by the addition of a larger bead between its branches, I discovered this design. Further exploration expanded the original concept into a semi-circular hollow form which could hold something of a similar size. A coin pearl could be cupped and held with two semicircular forms stitched together. Aha! There it was. Many of my beading discoveries are through just playing around and exploring the many facets of each beading stitch. The addition of the Swarovski margarita flower crystal adds subtle sparkle.

MATERIALS

EARRINGS

4 g topaz AB 15º Japanese seed beads (MC)

1 g bronze metallic 15º Japanese seed beads (AC)

1 g brown iris 11º Japanese seed beads

4 tabac 6mm Swarovski 3700 margarita beads

2 cream 11mm coin freshwater pearls

2 faceted 6x10mm carnelian drops

4 vermeil 2x2mm cornerless cubes

2 gold-filled ear wires with citrine stone inlay

16" (41 cm) of gold-filled 24-gauge wire

6 lb FireLine

Size 12 beading needles

BRACELET

10 g topaz AB 15º Japanese seed beads (MC)

3 g bronze metallic 15º Japanese seed beads (AC)

3 g brown iris 11º Japanese seed beads

5 tabac 6mm Swarovski margarita beads

8 khaki 3mm Swarovski bicone beads

5 cream 11mm coin freshwater pearls

4 faceted 4x6mm carnelian rondelles

18 vermeil 2x2mm cornerless cubes

8 gold-plated 6mm bead caps with inset

20mm gold-filled toggle clasp

30" (76.5 cm) of gold-filled 24-gauge wire

6 lb FireLine

Size 12 beading needles

TOOLS

Chain-nose pliers

Round-nose pliers

Flush cutters

Beading mat

SIZE

Each Earring: 1.75" (4.5 cm). Bracelet: 7.5" (19 cm)

TECHNIQUE

Flat circular Ndebele, wrapped loops, picot, reverse picot

EARRINGS

FIRST MEDALLION SIDE

→1 Using 1 yd (91.5 cm) of FireLine, string eight 15° AC beads and tie into a ring with a square knot, leaving a 6 to 8" (15.5 to 20.5 cm) tail. Pass through counterclockwise (CCW) one bead from the knot **(Fig. 1)**.

→2 Pick up two 15° MC beads and pass down into the adjacent AC bead CCW, then up the next adjacent AC bead. Repeat three more times. Step up by passing up through the first AC bead and the first bead in the second row **(Fig. 2)**.

→3 The third row will be increased with an 11° bead. By adding a larger bead, further Ndebele rows will spread out. Pick up two 15° MC beads and pass down through the adjacent 15° MC bead CCW. Pick up an 11° bead and pass up through the next adjacent 15° MC bead. Repeat three more times. Step up by passing up through the first bead of the second and third rows **(Fig. 3)**.

→4 The fourth row is a regular Ndebele row. Pick up two 15° MC beads and pass down CCW through the adjacent 15° MC beads for two rows. Pass through the 11° bead and up through the adjacent 15° MC beads for two rows. Repeat three more times. Step up by passing up through the first bead of the third and fourth rows **(Fig. 4)**.

→5 On the fifth row, a picot is added to each of the four Ndebele points. Pick up three 15° MC beads and pass down CCW through the adjacent 15° MC beads for three rows. Pass through the 11° bead and up into the adjacent 15° MC beads for three rows. Repeat three more times. Pass under the thread from a previous pass and tie an overhand knot. Weave through several beads and make another overhand knot. Repeat twice, weave down into the Ndebele point and trim thread **(Fig. 5)**.

→6 With the tail end of thread, weave thread to Location 1 at the midpoint of an Ndebele point **(Fig. 6)**. Face the needle up and out from the center. Pick up a margarita and a 15° AC bead. Pass back through the margarita.

→7 The margarita needs to be locked into place and centered. To do this, pass under the thread from a previous pass, at the opposite end, in Location 2. Pass back through the margarita, the 15° bead, and back down through the margarita again.

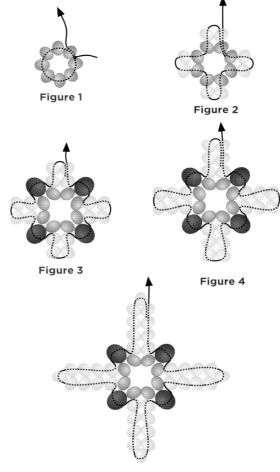

Figure 1

Figure 2

Figure 3

Figure 4

Figure 5

→8 Next pass under the thread at Location 3. Pass through the margarita, the 15° bead, and back down through the margarita.

→9 Pass under the thread at Location 4 to center the margarita. Tie an overhand knot.

→10 Weave up two beads into the Ndebele point and pass under the thread from a previous pass. Tie another overhand knot.

→11 Repeat Step 10 twice. Weave through three beads and trim thread from the inside of beadwork. Set aside.

TIPS

→ These medallions are very versatile and can be linked together in a multitude of ways for earrings, bracelets, or necklaces.

→ For a bracelet or necklace, only one side is embellished with a margarita bead for a more comfortable fit.

→ Square pearls can also be adapted for use in this design.

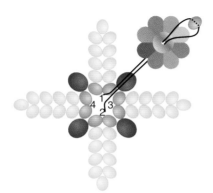

Figure 6

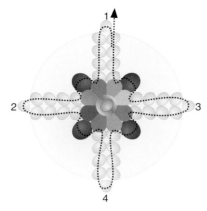

Figure 7

SECOND MEDALLION SIDE

→**12** Repeat all steps in the first medallion side except skip Step 5.

→**13** Attach the margarita as in Steps 6 to 11.

→**14** The two sides are joined together by sharing the center bead of the picot. The thread should be positioned exiting the first bead of the fourth row.

→**15** Pick up a 15° bead and pass CCW through the top bead of one of the picots on the first medallion side.

→**16** Pick up a 15° bead and pass down through the adjacent 15° beads for three rows.

→**17** Pass through the 11° accent bead and up into the adjacent 15° beads for three rows **(Fig. 7)**.

→**18** Repeat Steps 15 to 17 twice. Weave thread up the adjacent 15° beads for three rows.

→**19** Add the coin pearl. Pick up a 15° bead and pass CCW through the top bead of the last picot on the first medallion side.

→**20** Pick up a 15° bead and pass down through the adjacent 15° beads for three rows.

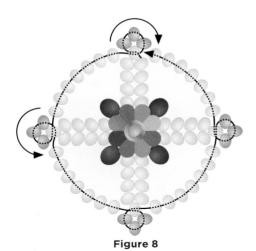

Figure 8

COMPLETING THE EARRING

→**26** Make two pearl Ndebele medallions.

→**27** With 4" (10.5 cm) of wire, make a wrapped-loop bail (p. 132) with the carnelian drops.

→**28** With 4" (10.5 cm) of wire, make a wrapped loop but add the ear wire before completing the wrap.

→**29** String a cube, the medallion, and a cube. Make a wrapped loop but before completing the wrap, add the drop made in Step 27.

→**30** Repeat Steps 27 to 29 for the other earring.

→**21** Pass through the 11° bead and up into the adjacent 15° MC beads for three rows. Pass under the thread from a previous pass and tie an overhand knot.

→**22** Pass through the center bead of the first picot. Pick up three 15° AC beads and pass back through the opposite end of the picot clockwise (CW). This is a reverse picot or a right-angle-weave link.

→**23** Pick up seven 15° MC beads and pass CCW through the center bead of the next picot. Depending on the 15° MC bead you select, you may need to string 7 to 9 beads. The beads should wrap around the edge of the coin pearl without rolling over **(Fig. 8)**.

→**24** Repeat Steps 22 and 23 three more times.

→**25** Reinforce around all beads added in Steps 22 to 24. Pass under the thread from a previous pass and tie an overhand knot. Weave through several beads and make another overhand knot. Repeat twice, weave down into one of the Ndebele points, and trim thread.

BRACELET

FIRST MEDALLION SIDE

→**31** Repeat Steps 1 to 11.

SECOND MEDALLION SIDE

→**32** Repeat Steps 1 to 4. Weave the tail thread into the bead-work, pass under thread from a previous pass, and tie an overhand knot. Weave through several beads and make another knot. Repeat twice and trim thread. There is no need to add the margarita embellishment because the medallion will not lie properly on the wrist if both sides are embellished.

→**33** The two sides are joined together by sharing the center bead of the picot. The thread should be positioned exiting the first bead of the fourth row.

→**34** Repeat Steps 14 to 25.

COMPLETING THE BRACELET

→**35** Make five pearl Ndebele medallions.

→**36** With 2.5" (6.5 cm) of wire, make a wrapped loop. String a cube, a crystal, a bead cap, a carnelian rondelle, a beadcap, a crystal, and a cube. Complete the link with another wrapped loop. Repeat for three additional links.

→**37** With 4" (10.5 cm) of wire, make a wrapped loop around one end of the toggle. String a cube, a medallion, and a cube. Make sure the wire is strung with the margarita bead side facing up. Make a wrapped loop but before completing the wrap, add one of the links made in Step 36.

→**38** With 4" (10.5 cm) of wire, make a wrapped loop but before completing the wrap, add the other side of the link connected in Step 37. String a cube, a medallion, and a cube. Make a wrapped loop but before completing the loop, add a second link made in Step 36.

→**39** Repeat Steps 37 and 38, connecting the medallions and links with the last medallion connected to the other end of the toggle.

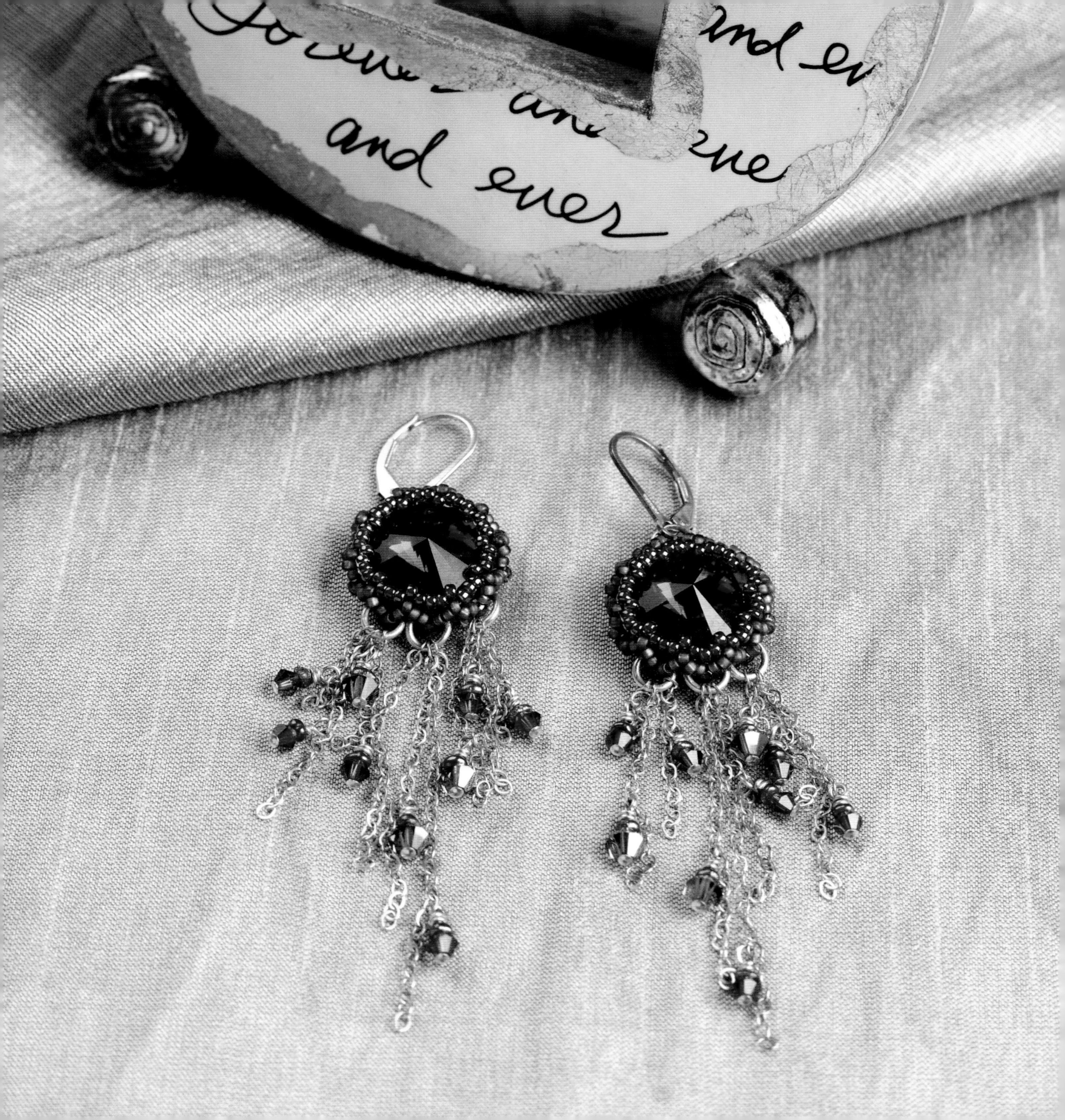
and ever

Netted Rivoli Chain
EARRINGS

I was first drawn to using rivoli rhinestones in my beadwork from
the "Crystal Collage" workshop I took with Marcia DeCoster. Since then
I've been playing around with different ways of encapsulating these
wonderful rhinestones, and I've had fun discovering playful ways
to use them in my beadwork. I enjoy mixing things up and regularly
add chain or wire elements to my beadwork. The tiered effect
created by the differing lengths of fine chain exudes a sense
of livelines as the earrings move with you.

MATERIALS

3 g matte silver-lined amethyst AB
15° Japanese seed beads (MC)

3 g topaz rose AB 15° Japanese seed
beads (back of bezel) (AC A)

1 g fuchsia crystal-lined 15°
Japanese seed beads
(last two rows of bezel) (AC B)

1 g amethyst AB 11°
Japanese seed beads

2 amethyst 14mm Swarovski
rivoli rhinestones

6 fuchsia 3mm Swarovski
bicone beads

6 amethyst 3mm Swarovski
bicone beads

6 tanzanite satin 4mm Swarovski
bicone beads

18 fuchsia freshwater
pearls (optional)

18 gold-filled 1.5 (38 mm) head pins

20" (51 cm) of gold-filled 2mm
cable chain

8 gold-filled 5mm jump rings

2 gold-filled leverbacks

6 lb FireLine

Size 12 beading needles

TOOLS

Chain-nose pliers

Round-nose pliers

Flush cutters

Beading mat

SIZE

2" (5 cm) from bottom
of leverback

TECHNIQUE

Circular peyote, netting,
wrapped loop, picot

BEZELS

→**1** Using 1 yd (91.5 cm) of thread, pick up twenty 15° AC A beads and tie into a ring with a square knot. Pass through two beads and tie a half hitch knot. Repeat once more and trim tail thread **(Fig. 1)**.

→**2** Pass through two beads, pick up a 15° bead, and weave into every other bead of the ring. Step up on last stitch by weaving into the first bead added in this row. This creates three rows of circular peyote. There should be ten high beads **(Fig. 2)**.

→**3** Pick up three beads and weave into every high bead. This creates a picot. Step up on last stitch by weaving into the top bead of the first picot **(Fig. 3)**.

→**4** Switch to the 15° MC bead. Pick up three 15° beads and weave into the high bead of the second picot. Repeat nine times to connect all remaining picots **(Fig. 4)**.

TIP

→ These bezel rivoli rhinestones make great components for a bracelet or necklace and can be used as buttons and flower centers. This is a method of encapsulating rhinestones that will definitely add to your beading repertoire.

Figure 1

Figure 2

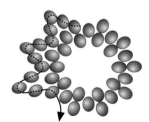

Figure 3

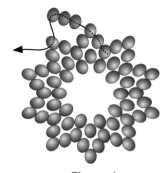

Figure 4

5 Weave into the first set of three beads added in Step 4. Treat the three beads as one element. Weave one 11° bead in between each of the three-bead sets. There should be ten 11° beads added **(Fig. 5)**.

6 Weave to the next 11° bead and pick up five 15° MC beads to create a picot. Repeat nine times. Weave into the first 11° bead and step up into the top (third) picot bead **(Fig. 6)**.

7 Insert the rivoli into the bezel. Switch to the 15° AC B bead. Pick up three 15° beads and weave into the third bead of the second picot created in Step 6. Repeat nine times **(Fig. 7)**.

8 Tighten the bezel by adding one 15° bead in between each three-bead set added in Step 7. Treat the three beads as one element. Weave through all beads in the last two rows once more to tighten. With the proper tension, the bezel will appear scalloped. This is more visible when the last two rows are the same color.

9 Weave thread down into the back of beadwork. Pass under the thread of a previous pass and tie an overhand knot. Repeat twice and trim thread.

10 Repeat Steps 1 to 9 for the second rivoli.

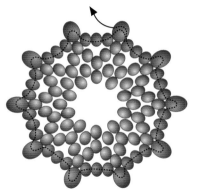

Figure 5

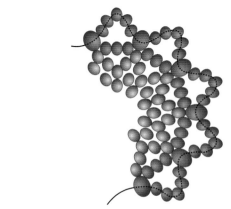

Figure 6

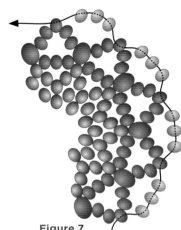

Figure 7

CHAIN LENGTHS

Right:

1st ring: 10, 20, 15 links
2nd ring: 20, 30, 25 links
3rd ring: 15, 20, 10 links

Left:

1st ring: 10, 20, 15 links
2nd ring: 25, 30, 20 links
3rd ring: 15, 20, 10 links

Figure 8: Right

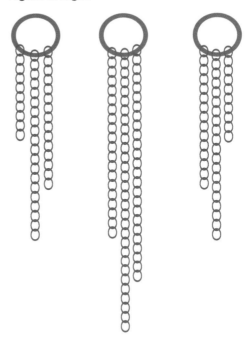

Figure 8: Left

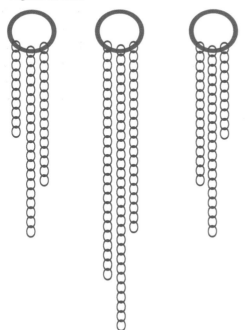

DANGLE LOCATIONS

Right:

1st ring: 3, 10, 5 links
2nd ring: 13, 20, 8 links
3rd ring: 5, 10, 3 links

Left:

1st ring: 3, 10, 5 links
2nd ring: 8, 20, 13 links
3rd ring: 5, 10, 3 links

CRYSTAL LOCATIONS

Crystals are arranged in the following order from left to right:

1. 3mm MC

2. 4mm

3. 3mm AC

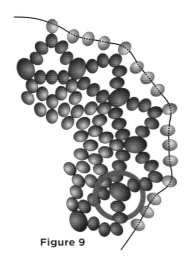

Figure 9

ADDING THE CHAIN DANGLES

Follow the diagram **(Fig. 8)** to attach the chain to the earrings. This will ensure that the earrings are mirror images.

↳**11** For each pair of earrings, cut the following: Four 10-links, four 15-links, six 20-links, two 25-links, and two 30-links.

↳**12** Open the jump ring and slide three chain links as shown in **Fig. 8**, working left to right. Repeat with the other two jump rings.

↳**13** Loop the first jump ring over two adjoining five-bead picot stitches on the rivoli bezel, working left to right. Repeat for the other two jump rings **(Fig. 9)**.

↳**14** Pick up the crystals and pearls onto the head pins and make a loop but do not close the wrap. I like to make a preliminary loop and attach to the chain before completing the wrapped loop. This helps visualize if you like the dangle placement before committing yourself. Refer to **Fig. 8** for suggested dangle locations. The crystals are added in the following order from left to right: 3mm MC, 4mm, and the 3mm AC. Complete the wrapped loops.

↳**15** Connect the last jump ring to the bezel opposite of the center chain dangle. Before closing jump ring, slide in the leverback.

↳**16** Repeat for second earring, ensuring that the center chain dangle is a mirrored image to the first, as shown in **Fig. 8**.

Pearl Cascade
NECKLACE

I wanted to design a piece with floating flowers and pearls that a mother of the bride would wear on her daughter's wedding day. The use of different-shaped pearls added textural and dimensional interest. The graduated mother-of-pearl flower clusters add a touch of class, which balances the design. Having the necklace offset also creates a sense of random but controlled movement. The addition of crystals creates a subtle sparkle in an otherwise monochromatic palette. The three chain links with their pearl dangles create a fun and playful swing.

MATERIALS
48 crystal copper 3mm Swarovski bicone beads

48 cream 5mm freshwater pearls

6 cream 2x4mm keishi rondelle pearls

42 cream 6x8mm keishi drop pearls

21 cream 9x12mm keishi drop pearls

4 cream 20mm mother-of-pearl (MOP) flowers with center holes

2 cream 25mm MOP flowers with center holes

6 vermeil 4mm daisy spacers

102 vermeil 2x2mm cornerless cubes

6 vermeil 5mm star bead caps

48" (122 cm) of gold-filled cable chain (with 2mm links)

156" (396.5 cm) of 24-gauge gold-filled wire

54 gold-filled 2" (50 mm) head pins

21mm gold-filled 3-strand slider clasp

TOOLS
Chain-nose pliers

Round-nose pliers

Flush cutter

Optional: Necklace stand

SIZE
28" (71.5 cm) longest strand;
22" (56 cm) shortest strand

TECHNIQUE
Wrapped loops

TIPS

→ Building the necklace on a tall necklace stand will help you visualize and align the design much better.

→ Do not cut the wire into separate lengths. It will be easier to create each link from the wire and cut as each link is made.

CREATING THE BASE

It is easier to create the tiered effect and align the three strands first with the chains intact. The chain for each tier is cut at the end when we are ready to attach to the three strand slider clasp. By varying the quantity of pearl and crystal link elements in each of the three chains, a tiered effect is created.

→1 Cut the chain to three 16" (41 cm) lengths.

→2 With the wire, make eighteen wrapped links with the crystals.

→3 With the wire, make a wrapped loop but before completing the wrap, add one end of a 16" (41 cm) chain and then complete the wrap.

→4 String a cube, a small keishi drop, a large keishi drop, a small keishi drop, and a cube. Make a wrapped loop but before completing the wrap, add the link made in Step 3 and then complete the wrap.

→5 With the wire, make a wrapped loop but before completing the wrap, add the other end of the crystal link added in Step 4 and then complete the wrap.

→6 Repeat, adding pearl and crystal links as in Steps 4 and 5, until there are eight pearl and eight crystal links.

→7 With the wire, make a wrapped loop but before completing the wrap, add the other end of the last crystal link created and then complete the wrap.

→8 String a cube, a small keishi drop, a large keishi drop, a small keishi drop, and a cube. Make a wrapped loop but

before completing the wrap, add the other end of the 16" (41 cm) chain and then complete the wrap. This chain should result in about 28" (71.5 cm). There should be a total of nine pearl and eight crystal links with the end links as pearl links.

→9 Repeat Steps 3 to 8 with the next 16" (41 cm) chain, this time resulting in seven pearl and six crystal links. The first and last links are always pearl links. This chain should be about 25" (63.5 cm).

→10 Repeat Steps 3 to 8 with the last 16" (41 cm) chain, this time resulting in five pearl and four crystal links. This chain should be about 22" (56 cm).

ADDING THE MOP BEAD ACCENTS AND JOINING THE 3 CHAINS

→11 Each of the MOP flower beads are attached 1" (2.5 cm) away from the last link made to the chain at both ends. On the shortest and longest chain the smaller MOP flower is attached. On the center chain the largest MOP flower is attached.

→12 On one side of the shortest chain, with a 2" (50 mm) head pin, string a crystal, a bead cap facing up, a small MOP flower, and a daisy through the chain, 1" (2.5 cm) away from the last link made. Make a wrapped loop and fold over the loop onto the chain to lock into place.

→13 Repeat Step 12 with a small MOP flower on the opposite side of the shortest chain.

→14 Repeat Steps 12 and 13 with the two large MOP flowers on the center chain.

→15 Repeat Steps 12 and 13 with the last two small MOP flowers on the longest chain.

→16 The three chains should be aligned so the MOP flower of the shortest chain flows nicely into the flower of the center chain and so forth. Use a necklace stand to align the chains. Before moving forward, lay out the chains from the shortest outward to the longest chain. Make sure the flowers face forward.

17 With the remainder twenty-four crystals, use the 2" (50 mm) head pins to make dangle drops by making a wrapped loop on each.

18 Use a 2" (50 mm) head pin to string one cube from the inside outward through the shortest chain, about ¼" (1 cm) away from the farthest MOP flower connection.

19 String one 5mm pearl through the center chain. String another 5mm pearl through the last chain.

20 String a cube and make a wrapped loop but before completing the wrap, add a crystal dangle created in Step 17.

21 Repeat Steps 19 and 20 on the opposite side to secure the flowers.

22 Hereafter, Steps 19 and 20 are made ½" (1.5 cm) away from the original connections. To ensure that the links are even, you may want to count the links in every chain as you string. For my style of chain, the connections were made on the tenth link away from the previous connection.

23 Sixteen total connection links are made on one side (counting the original connection link behind the MOP flower clusters). Eight total connection links are made on the opposite side (counting the original connection link behind the MOP flower clusters). The reason there are more links on one side versus the other is that the necklace will be offset to add more visual interest.

CONNECTING THE SLIDER CLASP

24 Cut all three chains in the center of the remaining chain.

25 With 3" (8 cm) of wire, make a wrapped loop but before completing the loop, connect to the topmost ring on the slider clasp. String one cube, a keishi rondelle, and a cube. Make a wrapped loop but before completing the wrap, add the longest chain.

26 Repeat Step 25 with the center chain and then with the shortest chain.

27 Repeat Steps 25 and 26 on the opposite end of the slider clasp. The tricky part is to make sure the crystal dangles faced outward with no twists to the chain when you make the connections to the second side. Use the necklace stand for help again, if necessary.

V Scallop
NECKLACE

The elegant gem-encrusted necklace collars you may see
on Hollywood mavens were the inspiration for this piece. You can
create your own red carpet event with an elegant necklace to
spice up a simple evening dress. The recipe is clear: Swarovski
crystals for the sparkles, the pearls for a pinch of elegance, and the
scalloped edging for a touch of femininity. The "V" shape accentu-
ates the neckline, and the vintage button closure adds a bit of
old-world glamour to the necklace.

MATERIALS

10 g matte sage iris 11° Japanese
seed beads (MC)

5 g matte amethyst AB 11° Japanese
seed beads (AC)

5 g bronze metallic 15° Japanese
seed beads

2 g silver-lined lt. olive 1.5mm
Japanese cubes

77 tanzanite 4mm Swarovski bicone
beads

75 lilac 3x4mm freshwater pearls

14mm shank button

6 lb FireLine

Size 12 beading needles

TOOLS

Chain-nose pliers

Flush cutters

No-tangle thread bobbin

Beading mat

SIZE

19.5" (49.5 cm)

TECHNIQUE

Right-angle weave (RAW), scalloping

CREATING THE RAW LINKS

→1 Start with 4 yd (3.6 m) of FireLine. From the center of the thread, wrap half of the FireLine onto the bobbin. You will need to add new thread later, but this method will reduce the number of times new thread is needed.

→2 Pick up twelve 11° MC beads and tie into a circle with a square knot. This will create a four-sided RAW link with 3 beads on each side. Pass through through six beads CW away from the knot **(Fig. 1)**.

→3 Pick up nine MC beads and pass CCW through the last three beads from the previous link. Pass CCW through six beads and continue making thirty-seven links switching thread path to CW, then CCW, etc. There should be thirty-nine links.

→4 To create the "V" at the center of the necklace, pass through three additional beads to offset the orientation of the next link (These three beads are outlined in red on **Fig. 2**).

→5 Pass CW through nine beads and continue making the remaining thirty-eight RAW links, switching thread path to CCW, then CW, etc.

→6 Weave CW through nine beads to start the second row off of the first RAW row. Pick up nine MC beads and pass CCW through the adjoining three beads on the last link from the first row.

→7 Pass CW through three more beads. Pick up six MC beads and weave CW into the three beads adjoining from the first row and the three beads adjoining from the link just created.

→8 Pass CW through six beads on the second link and continue making thirty-five links switching thread path to CW, then CCW, etc. There should be thirty-seven links.

→9 Now the beading has to be offset again to compensate for the "V." Pass CCW through three additional beads. Pick up three MC beads and weave CW through the nine beads adjoining this link.

→10 Weave CW through the three beads added in Step 9 and CCW through three beads on the next link from the first row. Continue making the remaining thirty-seven RAW links, switching thread path to CCW, then CW, etc.

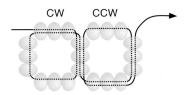

Figure 1

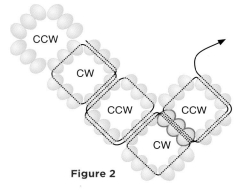

Figure 2

TIPS

→ Because a shank button is used, this necklace can easily be flipped over and worn on the less ornate side.

→ Although pearls and crystals are used for the embellishments, you can also use any beads that are 4mm in size.

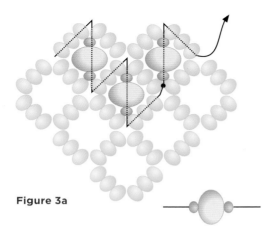

Figure 3a

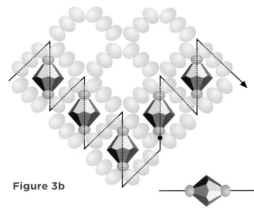

Figure 3b

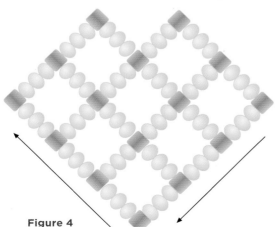

Figure 4

EMBELLISHING THE RAW LINKS

→**11** Starting from the inner second RAW row, pick up a 15° bead, a pearl, and a 15° bead diagonally to the opposite side of the RAW link. Pass through the opposite diagonal corner with the needle facing the same direction as the original thread path through three beads. Continue adding embellishments in this sequence for the remainder links until reaching the "V" section.

→**12** The thread will need to be re-oriented to turn the embellishment in the "V" section. To switch the beading orientation, the easiest method is to pass under the thread from a previous pass **(Fig. 3a)**.

→**13** Continue embellishing this row to mirror the direction on the opposite side.

→**14** Pass under the thread from a previous pass and continue embellishing in the same orientation for the lower RAW row. Replace the pearl with a crystal instead.

→**15** Pick up a 15° bead, a crystal, and a 15° bead diagonally to the opposite side the RAW link. Pass through the opposite diagonal corner with the needle facing the same direction as the original thread path through three beads. Continue adding embellishments in this sequence for the remaining links until reaching the "V" section.

→**16** The thread will need to be re-oriented to turn the embellishment in the "V" section. To switch the beading orientation, the easiest method is to pass under the thread from a previous pass **(Fig. 3b)**.

→**17** Continue embellishing this row to mirror the direction on the opposite side.

→**18** The back of the necklace will also be embellished to make the necklace more substantial. You can leave it as is, if you wish. In the sample, four 11° AC beads are woven diagonally in the opposite direction from the surface embellishments. Repeat Steps 11 to 17 on the opposite side of the necklace with four AC beads as the embellishment beads.

→**19** In each of the RAW links there will be an exposed corner. A 1.5mm Toho square bead is stitched in between these gaps on the right side of the necklace. There should be three rows of gaps that will be covered, leaving the three gaps on either side of the necklace ends unembellished to allow space for adding the shank button and loop later **(Fig. 4)**.

→**20** After adding the cubes, weave off all loose ends of thread into beadwork with several half hitch knots and trim thread.

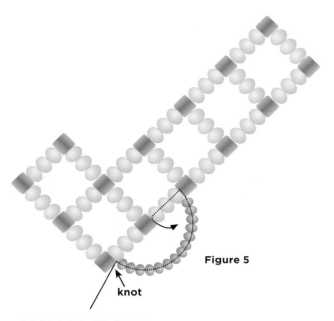

Figure 5

knot

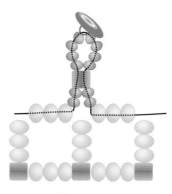

Figure 6

SCALLOP EDGING

→**21** On the bottom RAW row, a scallop edging will be added with 15° beads. Start with 3 yd (2.8 m) of FireLine. From the center, wrap half of the FireLine onto the bobbin.

→**22** Working from the center of the lower "V" row, pass under the existing thread path and tie an overhand knot at location shown **(Fig. 5)**. String fourteen 15° beads and weave back through the opposite end of the three MC beads in the next adjacent RAW link. The thread should be facing the opposite direction of original path.

→**23** Repeat this sequence until thirty-eight loops have been created on one side.

→**24** On the last link on this side, the thread path will have to be reversed to use the excess thread for making the button loop. Pass under the thread of a previous pass and tie an overhand knot to make turns. Pass back through the same three MC beads of the RAW link of the last loop.

→**25** Weave CCW through three MC beads of the same RAW link. The thread should be exiting from the center of the two rows of RAW.

→**26** Unwind the remaining FireLine from the bobbin. Weave though the center cube of the "V." Pass under the thread and tie an overhand knot to mirror Step 22.

→**27** Repeat Steps 22 and 23 for the opposite side to mirror the scallops previously made.

→**28** On the last link on this side, the thread path will have to be reversed to use the excess thread for stitching the shank button. Pass under a previous thread pass and tie an overhand knot to make turns. Pass back through the same three MC beads of the RAW link of the last loop.

→**29** Weave CW through three MC beads of the same RAW link. The thread should be exiting from the center of the two rows of RAW.

ADDING THE SHANK BUTTON

→**30** Pick up two 15° beads, a cube, eight 15° beads, and the shank button. Pass back through the cube.

→**31** Pick up two 15° beads and pass through the three adjacent MC beads from the inner row of RAW links **(Fig. 6)**.

→**32** Pass under the thread at the corner to turn work so the button shank can be reinforced. Pass through the three MC beads just passed through. Weave through all beads strung from Steps 30 and 31.

→**33** This time after exiting the two 15° beads on the end, weave into the three adjacent MC beads from the first row of RAW links.

→**34** Repeat Steps 32 and 33 once more. Pass under the thread at the corner, tie an overhand knot, weave thread into the beadwork, and trim thread.

ADDING THE PEYOTE BUTTON LOOP

→**35** Pick up two 15° beads, a cube, and thirty-one 15° beads. Weave back into the cube.

→**36** Pick up two 15° beads and weave into the three adjacent MC beads from the inner row of RAW links **(Fig. 7a)**. Test to make sure the loop fits over your button.

→**37** Pass under the thread at the corner to turn work so the button shank can be reinforced. Weave through the three MC beads just passed through. Pass through the two 15° beads, the cube, and the first 15° bead.

→**38** Pick up one 15° bead and pass through the third 15° bead on the loop. Continue picking up one 15° bead and passing through every other seed bead. You should have fifteen high beads **(Fig. 7b)**.

→**39** Weave into the cube and back down the other two 15° beads.

→**40** This time after exiting the two 15° beads on the end, weave into the three adjacent MC beads from the first row of RAW links.

→**41** Reinforce through the loop once more without adding any beads. Pass under the thread at the opposite corner from Step 40, tie an overhand knot, weave thread into the beadwork, and trim thread.

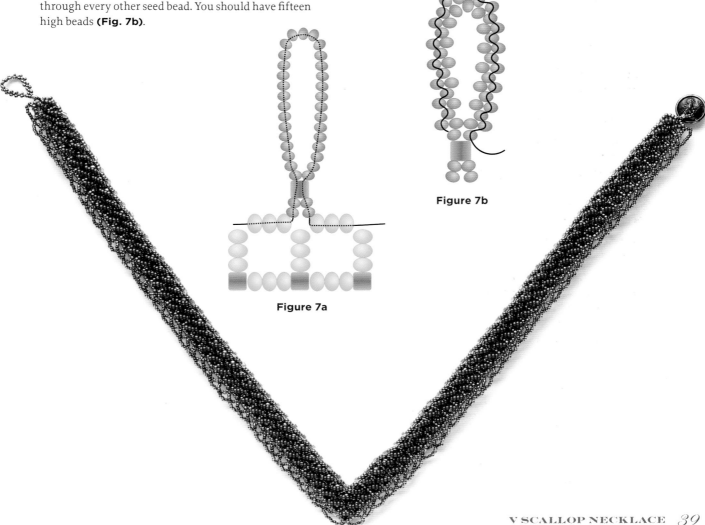

Figure 7a

Figure 7b

Mesh Pearl
BRACELET

I use freshwater pearls in just about any imaginable shape, size, and color in my jewelry designs. The elegant pearl dangles in this bracelet are accented by the wire mesh, which not only cushions the pearls but also creates volume and airiness. This bracelet is built on a graduated wire link design that I have been making for years. It can easily be shortened for a smaller wrist or elongated into a necklace by adding chain.

MATERIALS
49 lavender 6mm freshwater pearls

2 sterling silver 2x2mm cornerless cubes

45" (114.5 cm) of silver Italian 6mm wire mesh

45" (114.5 cm) of purple Italian 6mm wire mesh

36" (91.5 cm) of sterling silver 24-gauge wire

38 sterling silver 1.5" (38 mm) head pins

6mm sterling silver toggle clasp

TOOLS
Chain-nose pliers

Round-nose pliers

Flush cutter

GS Hypo Cement

SIZE
7.5" (19 cm)

TECHNIQUE
Wrapped loops

→ Do not cut the wire into separate lengths. It will be easier to create each link off of the entire length of wire and cut as each link is made.

→ Although pearls are used in this design, any leftover beads in a complementary palette can be used. If the beads are smaller, then more mesh would be required.

CREATING THE PEARL BRACELET

→1 String a pearl onto a head pin and make a wrapped loop with the loop being about 3mm in diameter. Make wrapped loops with thirty-eight pearls to create the dangle drops. Set aside.

→2 With the 24-gauge wire, make a loop and add one end of the toggle clasp onto the loop. Complete the wrapped loop.

→3 String a cornerless cube and make a loop. Add a pearl dangle and complete the wrapped loop.

→4 String a pearl on the wire and make a loop. Add the link made in the previous step with its pearl dangle rotated to the top of its loop. Add another pearl dangle and complete the wrapped loop. This method of adding the dangles ensures that the dangles hang in opposite directions.

→5 Repeat Step 4.

→6 Make a loop and add a pearl dangle. Add the link made in Step 5 with its pearl dangle rotated to the top of its loop and then add a second pearl dangle. Complete the wrapped loop. This connection link has a total of three pearl dangles **(Fig. 1)**.

→7 String a pearl on the wire and make a loop. Add a pearl dangle and add the link made in Step 6 in between its two dangles. Add another pearl dangle and complete the wrapped loop. This connection link has a total of four pearl dangles.

→8 Repeat adding pearl dangles in the following connection sequences (listed from the beginning): 2, 2, 3, 4, 4, 4, 4, 4, 4, 3, 2, and 2 until all pearl dangles have been added. Keep in mind the orientation of the dangles to ensure that they lay in opposing directions.

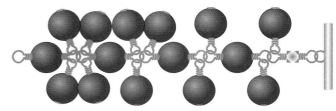

Figure 1

→9 On the last link, connect a cornerless cube to the other side of the toggle as in Step 2.

ADDING THE WIRE MESH

→10 Cut mesh into 2.5" (6.5 cm) strips. There should be eighteen strips of each color.

→11 The mesh is strung through the loops of each pearl dangle and knotted in the center. The third link from either side of the toggle has three dangles but only two mesh ribbons will be added. For the clusters of four pearl dangles, alternate the two mesh colors between same-connection loops.

→12 After all mesh has been tied, twist the ends and spread the strips to create leaflike shapes.

→13 Add a dab of GS Hypo Cement to the ends of each twist to prevent fraying. The GS Hypo Cement dries clear, so it won't interfere with the design. Trim excess ends with flush cutters as necessary after glue dries.

Ndebele Twist Band
WITH FLOWER CENTER

I collect design ideas from many places. It could be a catalog on furniture, linens, lamps, carpets, flowers, or even shoes. I was thumbing through a fashion magazine and saw an open-toe summer shoe with a twisted wrap on the front. The beader in me started imagining how I could execute a similar design with seed beads. I selected the Ndebele stitch for the bracelet band because it feels nice around the wrist and added a multilayered Ndebele floral as a focal point. Keeping the design in varying tones of the same hue created color harmony.

MATERIALS
15 g amethyst AB 11° Japanese seed beads (MC)

7 g bronze metallic 11° Japanese seed beads (AC A)

3 g periwinkle AB 11° Japanese seed beads (AC B)

1 g bronze metallic 15° Japanese seed beads

4 tanzanite 6mm Swarovski 5040 rondelles

1 periwinkle 6mm glass flower bead

1 gold-plated 10mm filigree bead cap

6 lb FireLine

Size 12 beading needles

TOOLS
Chain-nose pliers

Ruler

Flush cutters

SIZE
6.5" (16.5 cm)

TECHNIQUE
Flat and increasing Ndebele, even flat peyote, ladder stitch, picot

REGION 1: FLAT NDEBELE

The fitted band of this bracelet is divided into three regions. The first and third regions are the flat portions and are identical. After stitching the first region, the band will split in half to twist in the center. The third region reconnects the split from the second region back into a single flat band.

Figure 1

→1 Start with 1.5 yd (1.4 m) of FireLine. Pick up twelve 11° beads in the following sequence: an AC A, ten MC, and an AC A . Flip the strand so the last bead strung becomes the first bead in the ladder stitch.

→2 Ladder-stitch the beads to begin the first row of the Ndebele Band. Weave through the second bead CW, weave back into the first bead and down the second bead **(Fig. 1)**.

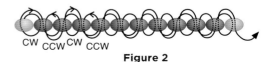

Figure 2

→3 Weave into the third bead CCW, weave back into the second bead and up the third bead.

→4 Repeat the ladder stitch, alternating CW and CCW, nine more times **(Fig. 2)**.

→5 Beading from right to left, with the thread exiting the AC A bead on the first row, pick up an AC A and a MC bead. Weave down into the second bead on the ladder row and up through the third bead on the ladder row.

Figure 3

→6 Pick up two MC beads and weave down into the fourth bead in the ladder row and up through the fifth bead on the ladder row.

→7 Repeat Step 6 three more times, weaving through respective ladder beads.

→8 Pick up a MC and an AC A bead for the last Ndebele stitch. The edge bead will always be an AC A bead. Weave down into the last bead on the ladder row **(Fig. 3)**.

Figure 4

→9 Weave up into the adjacent bead of this last pair on the ladder row and cross over one bead and up through the edge bead in the Ndebele stitch just created. The last stitch in each row steps up the beading into the next row **(Fig. 4)**.

→10 Continue beading flat Ndebele, Steps 4 to 9, for a total of thirty rows.

TIPS

→ If you wish to make a longer band, adjust the length of the two flat regions equally.

→ The center region should be no more than 2 inches or thirty rows of beading. Every inch stitched is fifteen rows.

REGION 2: THE SPLIT AND THEN TWIST

In this region, the band is split in two and then twisted before being joined back together. In order to achieve this, the first three Ndebele stitches will create the first strip beaded with the existing thread. A new thread will be added to separately bead the remaining three Ndebele stitches and create the second strip. Both strips will be beaded for thirty rows, then joined together in Region 3.

→**11** Pick up an AC A and a MC bead. Weave down into the second bead from the previous row. Weave up the third bead from the previous row **(Fig. 5)**.

→**12** Pick up two MC beads and weave down into the fourth bead from the previous row. Weave up the fifth bead from the previous row.

→**13** Pick up a MC and an AC A bead. Weave down into the sixth bead from the previous row. Turn the work as in Region 1, Step 9.

→**14** Repeat Steps 11 to 13 for a total of thirty rows. Set aside.

→**15** With 1 yd (91.5 cm) of FireLine, leave an 8" (20.5 cm) tail and add a new thread into the beadwork by going up the edge beads. Pass under the thread from a previous pass. Tie a square knot and weave up a few additional beads. Tie a half hitch knot. Weave thread up edge beads to continue beading the second strip.

→**16** Repeat Steps 11 to 13 for a total of thirty rows in the second strip.

→**17** The two strips are twisted by overlapping one strip over the other.

REGION 3: JOINING THE TWISTS

Using the original thread, the first row on the third region joins the two strips back into one band.

→**18** Pick up an AC A and a MC bead. Weave down into the second bead from the previous row. Weave up the third bead from the previous row **(Fig. 6)**.

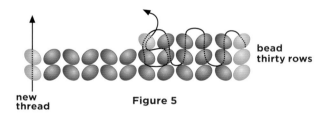

bead
thirty rows

new
thread

Figure 5

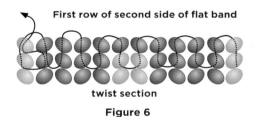

First row of second side of flat band

twist section

Figure 6

19 Pick up two MC beads and weave down into the fourth bead from the previous row. Weave up the fifth bead from the previous row.

20 Pick up two MC beads and weave down into the sixth bead from the previous row. Weave up the first bead in the second strip.

21 Pick up two MC beads and weave down into the second bead from the second strip. Weave up the third bead from the second strip.

22 Pick up two MC beads and weave down into the fourth bead from the second strip. Weave up the fifth bead from the second strip.

23 Pick up an MC and an AC A bead. Weave down into the sixth bead from the second strip.

24 Turn work as in Region 1, Step 9.

25 Repeat beading for the remainder of the thirty rows as in Region 1.

LOCKING THE TWO STRIPS DOWN

26 With the thread from the second strip, reinforce the connection of the two strips in the center by weaving through the first row of Region 3 once more.

27 Weave thread through several edge beads and pass under thread from a previous pass. Tie an overhand knot. Repeat twice and trim thread.

28 On the tail end of the added thread, weave thread to the center of the cross section where the two strips meet in the center. These two strips will have to be tacked down so that the flower can be added more easily later. There is no real methodology to this as long as no thread shows. This area will be covered by the Ndebele flower later.

29 Weave through several stitches and weave down through the top strip into the bottom strip.

30 Weave through several beads of the bottom strip and then back into the top strip with no thread showing.

31 Repeat Step 30 four to five times to secure the center. Then weave thread through several edge beads and pass under thread from a previous pass. Tie an overhand knot. Repeat twice and trim thread.

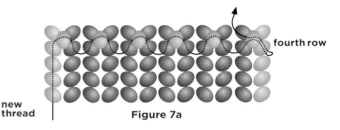

new thread

fourth row

Figure 7a

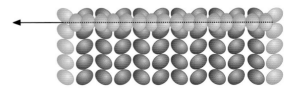

Figure 7b

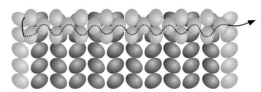

Figure 7c

THE CLASP CLOSURE

32 Weave a new thread onto one end of the band to exit out from the fourth row of beading. We will now transition to peyote stitch to make the decorative clasp ends for a more finished look.

33 Pick up an AC A bead on top of each of the Ndebele stitches to start peyote rows 1 and 2 **(Fig. 7a)**. There should be 6 beads added. After adding the last 11°, pass under a thread from a previous pass to turn the work.

34 Weave through the edge MC bead of the fourth row and through the last AC A bead just added.

35 Pick up two AC A beads and weave them in between each of the six beads added in Step 33. There should now be sixteen beads **(Fig 7b)**.

Figure 7d

Figure 8

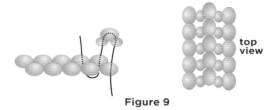

Figure 9

→**36** When you reach the original end, pass under the thread from a previous pass to turn the work.

→**37** Pick up an AC A bead and weave into the second bead from Step 35. Repeat weaving an AC A bead into every other bead. There will be eight high beads, and three rows of peyote have been completed **(Fig. 7c)**. Flip the band to the opposite side.

→**38** Repeat Steps 32 to 37.

→**39** Continue beading peyote stitch by beading into every high bead for a total of twenty rows. To check the row count, there should be ten beads on the outside edge.

→**40** Zipper the beading to the rows beaded on the first side. Circle the two end beads together. Weave through every high bead of each side and reinforce the other two end beads to finish zipping the sides **(Fig. 7d)**.

→**41** Weave the thread to exit out the first bead in the first peyote row. Pick up five 15° beads and weave into every other high bead of the first peyote row. There will be four picots created **(Fig. 8)**. On the last picot you will need to pass under the thread of the previous row to turn the work. Reinforce back through the picots to tighten and shape the embellishments.

→**42** The edge of the clasp band is still exposed. Weave the thread to exit out from the first edge AC A bead, in the first peyote row.

→**43** Pick up a 15°, an AC A, and a 15° bead and weave into the first AC A bead on the opposite side of the band. Weave up the adjacent edge AC A bead **(Fig. 9)**.

→**44** Repeat Step 43 four more times to cover this edge.

→**45** Repeat Steps 41 to 44 to add picots to the second inner side and to close up the second clasp edge.

→**46** Repeat Steps 32 to 45 on the second side of the band.

ADDING THE CRYSTAL TANZANITE BUTTONS

It is always easier to attach the button closures before making the loops. This way you can test the loops on an attached button to ensure proper sizing. Using two smaller buttons will distribute the closure tension evenly.

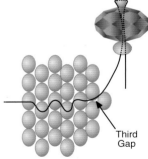

Figure 10

→**47** Weave into the fifth peyote row or count three outside beads down **(Fig. 10)**. Weave into the third high bead so the thread exits into the third gap of this row.

→**48** Pick up an AC A bead, a rondelle, and a 15° bead. Weave back through the rondelle, the AC A bead, and into the next high bead of this row.

→**49** Weave through five high beads in this row, until the thread exits into the third gap of this row looking from the opposite side.

→**50** Repeat Step 48 to add the second rondelle.

→**51** Weave to the end of the row and pass under the thread of a previous pass. Weave back to the button just added and reinforce the connection by weaving through all beads.

52 Weave to the first button added and reinforce the connection by weaving through all beads.

53 Repeat Steps 51 and 52 once more.

54 Weave thread to the end of the row and latch the thread to a previous pass. Tie an overhand knot, weave into the peyote band, and trim thread.

MAKING THE BUTTON LOOPS

55 Weave into the fifth peyote row or count three outside beads down. Weave into the third high bead so the thread exits into the third gap of this row.

56 Pick up an AC A and thirty-one 15° beads. Weave back into the AC A bead. Test the button closure to make sure it fits securely over the rondelle button created in the previous section **(Fig. 11a)**.

57 Weave through five high beads in this row, until the thread exits into the third gap of this row looking from the opposite side.

58 Repeat Step 56 to add the second loop.

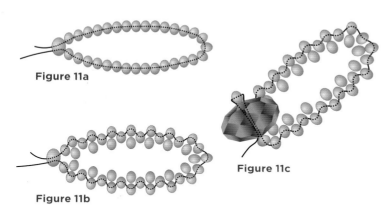

Figure 11a

Figure 11b

Figure 11c

59 Weave to the end of the row and pass under the thread of a previous pass. Weave back to the loop just added and reinforce the connection with a peyote row.

60 Weave through the AC A bead and the first 15° bead. Pick up a 15° bead and weave into the third 15° bead of the loop. Continue adding a 15° bead, weaving into every other bead in the loop. This should result in fifteen high beads **(Fig. 11b)**.

61 Weave to the first loop. Repeat Step 60.

62 Weave to the end of the row and pass under the thread of a previous pass. Weave back to the first loop to add the rondelle embellishments.

63 Pick up a rondelle, a 15° bead, and weave back into the rondelle **(Fig. 11c)**.

64 Weave to the other loop. Repeat Step 63.

65 Weave to the end of the row and pass under the thread of a previous pass. Return back to the rondelle just added and reinforce by weaving through all beads strung.

66 Weave to the first rondelle and reinforce by weaving through all beads strung.

67 Weave thread to the end of the row and latch the thread to a previous pass. Tie an overhand knot, weave into the peyote band, and trim thread.

MAKING THE FLOWER: CENTER LEVEL PETALS

68 Start with 1.5 yd (1.4 m) of FireLine. Pick up ten MC beads and create a ladder stitch as in the band.

69 Join the first and tenth bead into a ring by weaving up the first bead and back down the tenth bead **(Fig. 12)**.

70 Pick up two MC beads and weave CCW down into the second ladder bead. Weave up the third ladder bead.

71 Pick up two MC beads and weave CCW down into the fourth ladder bead. Weave up the fifth ladder bead.

72 Pick up two MC beads and weave CCW down into the sixth ladder bead. Weave up the seventh ladder bead.

73 Pick up two MC beads and weave CCW down into the eight ladder bead. Weave up the ninth ladder bead.

74 Pick up two MC beads and weave CCW down into the tenth ladder bead. Step up by weaving up the first ladder bead and the first bead strung in the second row **(Fig. 13a)**.

75 In the third row, the Ndebele stitch will be increased by adding an AC B bead in between each of the Ndebele stitches. Pick up two MC beads and weave CCW down the second bead of the second row. Before weaving up the next Ndebele stitch, pick up an AC B bead and weave up the third bead of the second row. You can use one color, but the

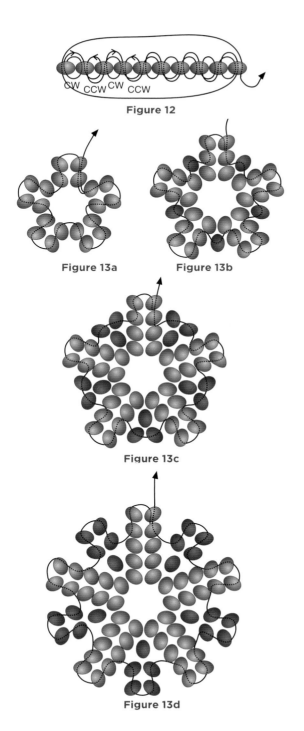

Figure 12

Figure 13a

Figure 13b

Figure 13c

Figure 13d

contrasting color will allow you to distinguish where the increases occur and also give the flower dimension. Repeat four more times so that there are five single beads between each of the Ndebele stitches. Step up on the last Ndebele stitch **(Fig. 13b)**.

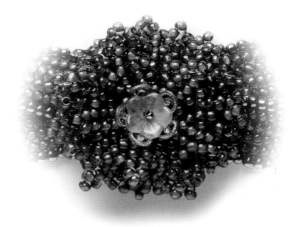

→**76** In the fourth row, two AC B beads are added on top of the AC B bead added in Step 75. Pick up two MC beads and weave CCW down the second bead of the third row. Before weaving up the next Ndebele stitch, pick up two AC B beads and weave up the third bead of the third row. These two AC B beads should be right over the AC B bead added in the third row. Repeat for four more times so that there are two AC B beads between each of the Ndebele stitches. Step up on the last Ndebele stitch **(Fig. 13c)**.

→**77** In the fifth row, the two AC B beads added previously will be treated as an Ndebele stitch. The flower petals will flare into having ten points. Pick up two MC beads and weave CCW down the second bead of the fourth row. Weave up the first AC B bead of the two bead increase, treating this as a regular Ndebele stitch. Pick up two AC B beads and weave down the second AC B bead of the two bead increase. Repeat four more times, resulting in ten Ndebele stitches **(Fig. 13d)**.

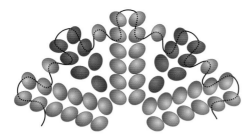

Figure 13e

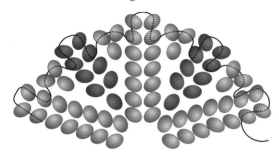

Figure 13f

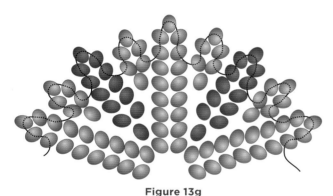

Figure 13g

→78 Repeat Steps 75 and 76, adding increases on the outside edges of the MC beads **(Figs. 13e and 13f)**.

→79 On the eighth and final row, instead of beading a regular Ndebele row, we will finish the floral points by making a picot with the respective color. There should be twenty points. Again, treat the two bead increases as if they were regular Ndebele stitches. Pick up three MC beads and weave down into the second bead from the seventh row and up the adjacent. Repeat nineteen more times, switching to the AC B beads for creating the picots, as necessary **(Fig. 13g)**.

TOP LEVEL PETALS

→80 The top level is beaded on top of the center petals. Weave down to the center of the flower through one of the Ndebele points. Weave up one bead with the thread exiting from the ladder-stitch row facing away from the center. The AC B beads will alternate in place of the MC beads used in the center level and vice versa **(Fig. 14)**.

→81 Repeat Steps 70 to 76 switching the MC beads for the AC B beads and vice versa.

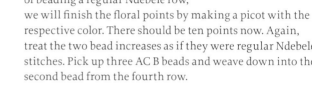

Figure 14

→82 In the fifth and final row, instead of beading a regular Ndebele row, we will finish the floral points by making a picot with the respective color. There should be ten points now. Again, treat the two bead increases as if they were regular Ndebele stitches. Pick up three AC B beads and weave down into the second bead from the fourth row.

→83 Repeat Step 82 nine more times, switching to the MC beads for creating the picots, as necessary. To spread the petal out, between the AC B and MC picots, an AC B bead will be added in between them.

BOTTOM LEVEL PETALS

→84 The bottom level is beaded below the center petals and begins the same way as the top level. Flip the flower over with the top level facing down. Weave down to the center of the flower through one of the Ndebele points. Weave up one bead with thread exiting from the ladder-stitch row facing away from the center. The AC B bead will alternate in place of the MC beads used in the center level and vice versa **(Fig. 14)**.

→85 Repeat Steps 70 to 78 from the center petal section, switching the MC beads for the AC B beads and vice versa.

→86 In the eighth row, the two beads added in the previous step will be treated as an Ndebele stitch. Bead a regular Ndebele row.

→87 On the ninth and final row, instead of beading another regular Ndebele row, we will end and finish the floral points by making a picot with the respective color. There should be twenty points. Pick up three AC B beads and weave down into the second bead from the eighth row and up the adjacent bead. Repeat nineteen more times, switching to the MC beads for creating the picots, as necessary. To spread the petal out, between the AC B and MC picots, an AC B bead will be added in between them.

STITCHING THE FLOWER TO THE BAND

→88 After the lower level of the Ndebele flower has been completed, weave down to the center of the flower. Weave thread coming out of the flower with the top-level petals facing you.

→89 Pick up the bead cap so that it is facing up. Pick up the flower bead and a 15° bead **(Fig. 15)**. Weave back down the flower and bead cap.

→90 The embellishment beads need to be locked into place and centered. To do this, pass under the thread from a previous pass, at the opposite end, in Location 2. Weave back up into the bead cap, flower, and the 15° bead. Weave back down the sequence. Next, pass under the thread at Location 3. Weave back up a third time and back down. Lastly, pass under the thread at Location 4 to center the embellishments. Tie an overhand knot **(Fig. 15)**.

→91 With the thread exiting out the center of the flower from the bottom, the flower will be attached to the center of the bracelet. "X" marks the spot in the twist, and this is where the flower will be tacked down. There is no real methodology to this as long as no thread shows.

→92 Weave through both layers of the twist section. Weave through several beads of the bottom strip and then back into the top strip. Weave into a few beads on the bottom row of the flower.

→93 Repeat Step 92 four to five times to secure the center. Then weave thread through several edge beads and pass under thread from a previous pass. Tie an overhand knot. Repeat twice and trim thread.

Figure 15

Bohemian Drop
EARRINGS

The antique brass filigree findings in these earrings conjure impressions of a bygone era. The flexible design could appear Edwardian, Victorian, or art nouveau. The earring design is a building block for the festoon necklace featured on page 68, using elements and findings from Vintaj Natural Brass Company. It was not difficult to be inspired by these findings. Like a well-worn, treasured piece of heirloom jewelry, these earrings add a piece of history to a modern design. A filigree wrap encases a coin pearl adding a tasteful element to an already classy design with a bohemian feel.

MATERIALS
1 g bronze metallic 15° Japanese seed beads

1 g chartreuse AB 11° Japanese seed beads

2 cream 12mm freshwater coin pearls

4 crystal copper 3mm Swarovski bicone beads

2 purple luster 9x10mm oval faceted glass beads

6 green luster 3x4mm Czech firepolished rondelles

2 antique 20x20mm square brass filigree

2 antique 12mm brass filigree bead caps

2 antique 4.75mm brass jump rings

2 antique brass leverback earring findings

6 lb FireLine

Size 12 beading needles

TOOLS
Chain-nose pliers

Optional: Old wooden ruler or dowel

Flush cutters

Beading mat

SIZE
2" (5 cm) (measured from jump ring)

TECHNIQUES
Right-angle weave, reverse picot, picot

CREATING THE BOHEMIAN DROPS

→1 With the square filigree, hold a coin pearl at center with index finger and thumb. Start the wrap on each of the four corners by bending slightly with pressure on your beading mat. Once started, use your chain-nose pliers to complete the wrap and carefully secure the coin pearl, ensuring its hole is centered between two folds for beading later. Repeat with other coin pearl. Use a wooden surface to burnish further, as necessary. Set aside for attachment in later steps.

→2 Start with 24" (61 cm) of FireLine. Pick up a rondelle, 15°, 11°, and 15° beads. Pass back through the rondelle, creating a picot and leaving a 5" (13 cm) tail thread **(Fig. 1)**.

→3 Pick up a 15°, rondelle, 15°, 11°, and 15° beads. Pass back through the second rondelle, creating another picot **(Fig. 2)**.

→4 Repeat Step 3 **(Fig. 3)**.

→5 Pick up a 15° bead and pass up through the opposite end of the first rondelle, so the picots are on the outer edge of each of the rondelles. Weave through all beads added in Step 2 **(Fig. 4)**.

→6 Pick up two 15°, one 11°, and two 15° beads and pass through all picot beads on the second rondelle **(Fig. 5)**.

→7 Repeat Step 6 twice. Weave to the 11° bead of the first picot **(Fig. 6)**.

→8 Pick up three 15° beads and pass through the opposite end of the 11° bead to create a reverse RAW picot **(Fig. 7)**.

→9 Weave to the next 11° bead and repeat Step 8 five times.

Figure 1

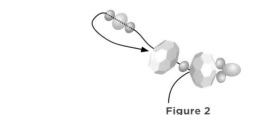

Figure 2

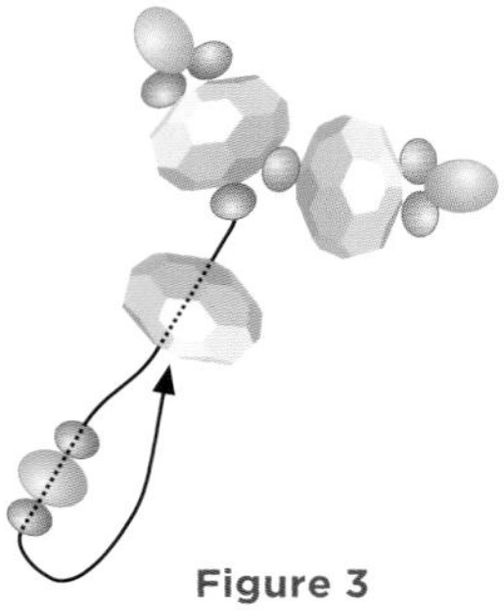

Figure 3

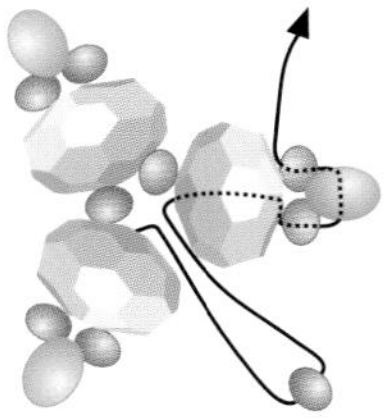

Figure 4

Figure 5

TIPS

→ A second 15° color bead may be added to the center of the medallion and on the tips of the crystal embellishments for added visual interest.

→ Use a wooden dowel or ruler to burnish the bead cap and filigree wrap without damage to the metal (p. 13).

Figure 6

Figure 7

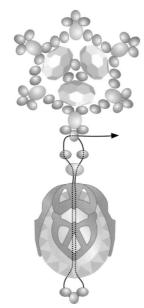

Figure 8

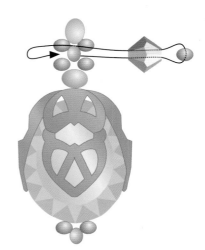

Figure 9

→**10** Weave up to the center bead of the first picot created. Pick up one 15°, one 11°, the bead cap, oval bead, and three 15° beads. Pass back through the oval, the bead cap, and the 11°. Pick up another 15° bead and pass back through the opposite end of the picot bead **(Fig. 8)**.

→**11** Pick up a crystal and 15° bead. Pass back through the crystal, into the opposite end of the picot bead, through the last bead of the picot sequence, and through the 11° bead **(Fig. 9)**.

→**12** Weave through all beads added in Step 10 to reinforce.

→**13** Pass under the thread from a previous pass and tie an overhand knot. Repeat twice and trim thread.

Figure 10

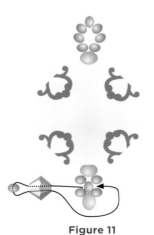

Figure 11

14 With the 5" (13 cm) tail thread, pass through the closest 15° AC bead in the center, into the rondelle. Weave thread to the center picot opposite of the oval bead added in Step 10.

15 Pick up one 15° MC, one 11°, coin pearl, one 11°, and seven 15° MC beads. Pass back through the 11° bead to create a connection loop, through the pearl, and 11° bead. Pick up another 15° MC bead and pass back through the opposite end of the picot bead **(Fig. 10)**.

16 Repeat Step 11 to add another crystal embellishment ensuring that both crystals are facing the same direction **(Fig. 11)**.

17 Weave through all beads added in Step 15 to reinforce.

18 Repeat Step 13.

19 Attach the earring assembly to the leverback finding with a jump ring.

20 Repeat Steps 2 to 18 for the other earring.

Rivoli Y Drop

NECKLACE

I enjoy finding different ways to bezel-set rhinestones. Rhinestones come in every shape, color, and size, in modern or vintage selections, and are a versatile design element to incorporate into beadwork. The Swarovski rivoli rhinestone is the easiest rhinestone to learn on because it is round and uniform in shape. It is much easier to bezel-set a round rhinestone, cabochon, or bead than one that is another shape. The "Y" necklace is an updated interpretation of Victorian jeweled necklaces worn by aristocratic ladies of the court.

MATERIALS

5 g matte cranberry fuchsia AB 11° Japanese seed beads

20 g purple luster 15° Japanese seed beads (MC)

7 g bronze metallic 15° Japanese seed beads (AC A)

7 g cranberry fuchsia AB 15° Japanese seed beads (AC B)

1 g purple iris 15° Japanese seed beads (AC C)

17 light vitrail 14mm Swarovski rivoli rhinestones

9x15mm light vitrail faceted Czech crystal drop

8° purple iris Czech drop beads

54 purple iris 3mm Czech firepolished beads

6 lb FireLine

Size 12 beading needles

TOOL

Chain-nose pliers

Flush cutters

SIZE

19" (48.5 cm)

TECHNIQUES

Circular peyote, right-angle weave

RIVOLI BEZEL BASE

→**1**   Start with 1 yd (91.5 cm) of FireLine. Pick up four 15° MC beads and tie into a circle with an overhand knot. Leave a 6" (15.5 cm) tail. This will create the first RAW link. Pass through two MC beads CW away from the knot **(Fig. 1a)**.

→**2**   Pick up three MC beads CCW into the opposite end of the second bead strung in the first link. Weave thread CCW through two beads and continue making seventeen more links, switching thread path to CW, then CCW, etc. There should be nineteen links.

→**3**   Join the nineteenth link to the first link by picking up one MC bead (A in **Fig. 1a**) CW into the respective side bead of the first link (or the fourth bead). Pick up another MC bead (B in **Fig. 1a**) and weave into the respective side bead of the nineteenth link. This will join the RAW links into a circle with twenty links.

→**4**   Flatten the ring with your fingers and switch to peyote stitch.

→**5**   Pass through the three beads along the existing thread path CCW until the thread exits one of the top beads in the RAW sequence **(Fig. 1b)**. It will be difficult to distinguish the step up in the last stitch of the peyote row, so count out twenty MC beads and the last bead left over will be the step up.

→**6**   Pick up a MC bead and pass through the next high bead on the RAW base **(Fig. 2)**. Continue adding a MC bead to every high bead on the RAW base nineteen more times. On the last bead step up by passing through the first bead in this row again.

TIPS

→ When working with size 15° seeds in peyote, it may get confusing where to step up as the beads are so tiny. Pre-count the beads in each row, and when you've reached the last bead, it's time to step up to the next row.

→ Beaded rivolis make wonderful button closures where you just want a little sparkle. They are also great for making drop earrings with chain.

Figure 1a   **Figure 1b**

Figure 2

Figure 3a

Figure 3b

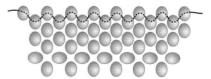

Figure 3c

7 Repeat Step 6 for three more peyote rows **(Figs. 3a–3c)**. Continue to hold beadwork flat while beading, so the result is a flat disc.

8 We are now in the sixth row. Pick up three 15° beads in the following sequence: AC A, MC, and AC A, to make a picot into every other high bead of the peyote row **(Fig. 4)**. This will decrease the disc so that the rivoli will be encapsulated once it is added to the bezel cup.

9 Repeat Step 8 nine more times to complete the round.

10 Pass the thread through the first two beads of the next picot, with the thread exiting the MC bead.

11 Pick up three AC A beads and make a RAW stitch by passing through the MC bead of the picot again. I call this stitch a reverse picot **(Fig. 5)**.

12 Repeat Steps 10 and 11 nine more times.

13 Pass through the beads along the existing thread path until the thread is exiting out of the high bead in the next reverse picot. This should be the third bead.

14 Insert a rivoli and close up the bezel by weaving an AC A bead in between each of the ten reverse picots created in Steps 11 and 12 **(Fig. 6)**. Weave through beads once more to tighten the bezel.

15 With the thread from the tail end, weave through the RAW beads of the first row without adding any beads. Pass under the thread from a previous pass and tie an overhand knot. Tighten stitch with a second row of enforcement. This will further cup the bezel so the rivoli is locked into place. Pass through several beads and secure with an overhand knot. Repeat twice more and trim thread.

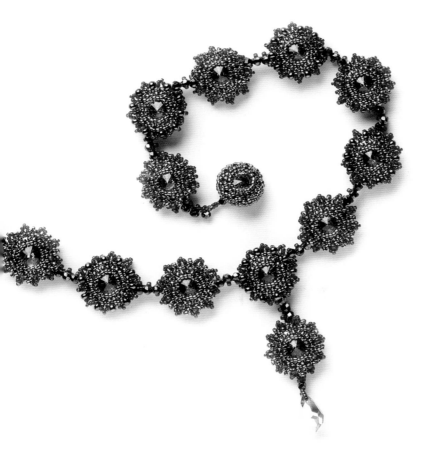

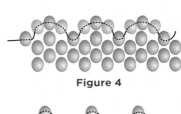

Figure 4

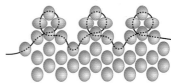

Figure 5

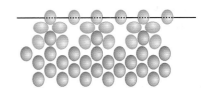

Figure 6

BUTTON CLOSURE

The button closure is an unembellished bezel with an added shank. Follow all steps in making the bezel base.

16 Continue from Step 15 but do not trim the excess thread off of the tail end.

17 Pick up nine MC beads and pass under the thread from a previous pass, on the opposite side. There should be ten beads in between the shank on either side since we originally began with twenty RAW links.

18 Pass back through the nine beads to reinforce. Pass under the thread from a previous pass.

19 Pass through two beads in the bottom row, in the opposite direction of the original thread path. Pass under the thread from a previous pass and pass back through the two beads and through the nine beads on the shank. **(Fig. 7)** Pass under the thread from a previous pass and tie an overhand knot. Weave through a few beads and trim thread.

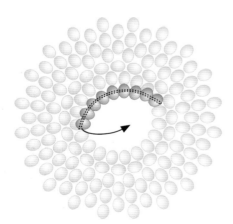

Figure 7

EMBELLISHMENT #1

20 Pass through the first AC A of a picot bead in the picot row. Pick up an 11° bead and pass through the next AC A bead of the same picot.

21 Pick up three AC A beads and pass through the first AC A bead of the next picot **(Fig. 8a)**.

22 Repeat Steps 1 and 2 nine more times, alternating between the two embellishments.

23 Weave down into the second peyote row, exiting out of a high bead. Pick up an 11° bead and pass through the next high bead, in between the three bead picot created in Step 21.

24 Pick up five AC B beads and pass through the next high bead, in between the beads added in Step 20. We are stitching in the gaps of the peyote row **(Fig. 8b)**.

25 Repeat Steps 23 and 24 nine more times, alternating between the two embellishments.

26 Excess thread will be used to create the links to connect two rivolis. Do not weave off thread.

27 Embellish a total of eight rivolis this way.

Figure 8a

Figure 8b

EMBELLISHMENT #2

28 Pass through the first AC A bead of the picot in picot row. Pick up a drop bead and pass through the second AC A bead of the same picot.

29 Pick up an AC C bead and pass through the first AC A bead of the next picot **(Fig. 9a)**.

30 Repeat Steps 28 and 29 nine more times, alternating between the two embellishments.

31 Weave down into the second peyote row, exiting out of a high bead. Pick up an 11° bead and pass through the next high bead, directly beneath a drop from Step 28.

Figure 9a

Figure 9b

32 Pick up five AC B beads and weave into the next high bead, beneath the bead added in Step 29. We are stitching in the gaps of the peyote row **(Fig. 9b)**.

33 Repeat Steps 31 and 32 nine more times, alternating between the two embellishments.

34 Excess thread will be used to create the links to connect two rivolis. Do not weave off thread.

35 Embellish a total of seven rivolis with this embellishment.

MAKING THE CONNECTIONS

The rivolis are connected in alternating sequence between embellishments 1 and 2, ending in a "Y" drop. Each rivoli was embellished the same on the last row. Two of the 11° beads will be used for the first and third sides of the RAW links connecting two rivolis. Each connection has three rows of RAW. The RAW is further embellished with a 3mm firepolished bead. Viewing from the back of the embellished rivoli, there are ten 11° beads. To ensure that the links are connected properly, there should be four 11° beads between the two connections (**Fig. 10a** shows only the 11° beads and the connecting right-angle weave links).

36 Starting with a rivoli with Embellishment #1, weave the thread into the closest 11° bead of the last row of embellishments.

37 Pick up three 11° beads and pass through the 11° bead on the rivoli to make the first RAW link.

38 Pass through two beads CW and pick up three 11° beads. Pass through the opposite end of the second bead strung from the first link.

39 Pass through two beads CW and pick up an 11° bead and pass through a 11° bead on a rivoli with Embellishment #2.

40 Pick up one 11° bead and weave into the opposite end of the second bead strung from the second RAW link **(Fig. 10b)**.

41 Reinforce by weaving through each of the RAW links in reverse direction. Once back to the first RAW link, embellish each link with a firepolished bead in a diagonal manner.

42 Pick up a firepolished bead and pass through the opposite diagonal corner of the first link with the needle facing the same direction as the original thread path **(Fig. 10c)**.

43 Repeat for the remaining two RAW links.

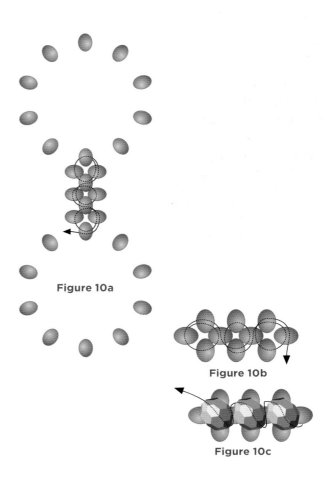

Figure 10a

Figure 10b

Figure 10c

44 Pass under the thread from a previous pass and reinforce the firepolished bead embellishments once more. Pass under the thread from a previous pass and weave thread into the rivoli base.

45 Repeat Steps 36 to 44 for seven links, alternating between the two different rivoli embellishments. Make sure there are four 11° beads separating the two opposite links on each rivoli **(Fig. 10a)**. After completing the seven links, verify that the first and seventh links are rivolis with Embellishment #1.

46 Repeat Steps 36 to 45 for the second side of the necklace. Make sure when embellishing the firepolished beads on the second strand to embellish in the opposite direction to Step 42.

CONNECTING THE Y RIVOLI FOCAL AND ADDING THE CRYSTAL DROP

The "Y" focal connection is made in the same manner as in the previous section but just at different locations. There will also be three connections instead of two and the locations will be offset from the center to create the "Y" drop **(Fig. 11a** outlined beads indicate connection locations).

47 With one of the seven-rivoli strands, weave the thread four 11° beads away from the opposite connection link.

48 Connect the last rivoli with Embellishment #2 as in previous steps.

49 Viewing from the bottom of the rivoli, weave the thread four 11° beads away CW from Step 47. There should be three beads between these connections.

50 Make a connection link onto the other seven-rivoli strand four beads away from the opposite connection link.

51 Viewing from the bottom of the rivoli, weave the thread three 11° beads away CW from Step 49. There should be two beads between these connections.

52 Make a connection link onto the last remaining rivoli with Embellishment #1.

53 Weave the thread five 11° beads away from the opposite connection made in Step 52. There should be four beads between these connections.

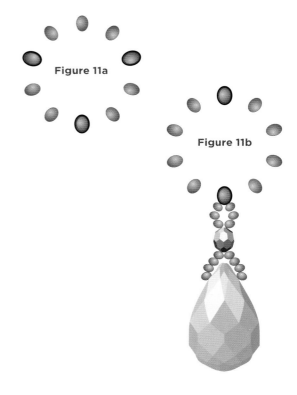

Figure 11a

Figure 11b

54 Pick up three AC B beads, a firepolished bead, four AC B beads, the crystal drop, and four AC B beads **(Fig. 11b)**.

55 Pass back through the firepolished bead. Pick up three AC B beads and pass through the opposite end of the 11° bead on the rivoli.

56 Reinforce two additional times by weaving through all beads strung in Steps 54 and 55.

57 Pass under the thread from a previous pass and tie an overhand knot. Weave the thread into the body of the rivoli base and trim thread.

CONNECTING THE RIVOLI BUTTON

58 Weave the thread five 11° beads away from the opposite connection link of the rivoli strand. There should be four beads between these connections.

59 Repeat Steps 37 and 38.

60 Pass through two beads CW and pick up three 11° beads. Weave into the opposite end of the second bead strung from the second link.

61 Repeat Steps 41 to 43.

62 Pass through the second bead strung in the third link. Pick up three AC B beads, a firepolished bead, seven AC B beads, and the rivoli button with shank **(Fig. 12)**.

63 Pass back through the firepolished bead and the first 15° bead. Pick up two 15° AC B beads and pass through the opposite end of the 11° bead.

64 Reinforce two additional times by passing through all beads strung in Steps 62 and 63.

65 Pass under the thread from a previous pass and tie an overhand knot. Weave the thread through the connecting RAW links, weave into the body of the rivoli, tie another overhand knot and trim thread.

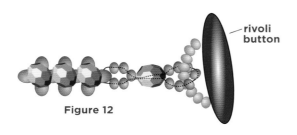

rivoli button

Figure 12

MAKING THE BUTTON LOOP

66 Weave the thread five 11° beads away from the opposite connection link of the rivoli strand. There should be four beads between these connections.

67 Repeat Steps 37 and 38.

68 Repeat Step 60.

69 Repeat Steps 41 to 43, embellishing in the opposite direction to the other side of necklace.

70 Pass through the second bead strung in the third link. Pick up three AC B beads, a firepolished bead, and forty-one AC B beads **(Fig 13a)**.

71 Repeat Step 63.

72 Reinforce through all beads up into the firepolished bead. The loop will be embellished further with two rows of peyote.

73 Weave through the first 15° bead. Pick up an AC B bead. Pass through the third bead of the loop to begin the peyote stitch.

74 Pick up an AC B, skip a bead on the base loop, and pass through the next bead on the loop.

75 Repeat Step 74 around the loop until you have twenty high beads **(Fig. 13b)**.

76 Pass through the firepolished bead, the 15° beads, and into the opposite end of the 11° bead.

77 Reinforce through all beads up into the firepolished bead. The loop will be embellished further with Czech drops. Pass through the first high bead without thread showing.

78 Pick up a Czech drop and pass through the next two high beads with no thread showing.

79 Repeat Step 16 until you have added ten drops **(Fig. 13c)**.

80 Pass through the firepolished bead, the 15° beads, and into the opposite end of the 11° bead.

81 Repeat Step 65.

Figure 13a

Figure 13b   **Figure 13c**

Quatrefoil Nouveau Festoon
NECKLACE

Festoon designs of the Victorian (1837 to 1901), and Edwardian (1901 to 1910) eras often featured swags of beads or chain that draped gracefully over the neckline. The centerpiece of this necklace is a floral glass drop from my Nouveau series, which captures the flowing, stylized flowers of the Art Nouveau era (1880 to 1914). The Vintaj Art Deco vine filigree wrap was chosen as it perfectly mimics the sweeping florals that seem to dance around the nouveau pendant. The quatrefoils from the Renaissance (fourteenth to seventeenth centuries) and Gothic Revival (nineteenth century) eras create a balance as beaded elements to the chain necklace.

MATERIALS
5 g brown iris 15° Japanese seed beads

1 g chartreuse AB 11° Japanese seed beads

4 off-white 12mm freshwater coin pearls

7 off-white 4.5mm freshwater pearls

11 crystal copper 3mm Swarovski bicone beads

12 sea green luster 3x4mm Czech firepolished rondelles

4 purple luster 9x10mm oval faceted glass beads

1 Nouveau 18x30 mm lampworked floral drop with sterling silver bail

2 antique 59x31mm Deco vines brass filigree wrap

4 antique 20x20mm square brass filigree

4 antique 12mm brass filigree bead caps

28 antique 4.75mm brass jump rings

17.5" (44.5 cm) of antique 3mm brass cable chain

1 antique 21x9mm brass swirl hook clasp

6 lb FireLine

Size 12 beading needles

TOOLS
Chain-nose pliers

Flush cutters

Optional: Liver of sulfur for antiquing bail on Nouveau drop

Optional: Old wooden ruler or dowel

Beading mat

SIZE
15.5" (39.5 cm)

TECHNIQUES
Right-angle weave, peyote, reverse picot

COIN PEARL DANGLES

→1 With the square filigree, hold a coin pearl at center with index finger and thumb. Start the wrap on each of the four corners by bending slightly with pressure on your beading pad. Once started, use your chain-nose pliers to complete the wrap and carefully secure the coin pearl, ensuring its hole is centered between two folds for beading later. Repeat with other coin pearl. Use a wooden surface to burnish further, as necessary. Set aside for attachment in later steps.

→2 Start with 24" (61 cm) of FireLine. Pick up a rondelle, 15°, 11°, and 15° beads. Pass back through the rondelle, creating a picot and leaving a 5" (13 cm) tail thread **(Fig. 1)**.

→3 Pick up a 15°, rondelle, 15°, 11°, and 15° beads. Pass back through the second rondelle, creating another picot **(Fig. 2)**.

→4 Repeat Step 3.

→5 Pick up a 15° bead and pass up through the opposite end of the first rondelle, so the picots are on the outer edge of each of the rondelles. Weave through all beads added in Step 2 **(Fig. 3)**.

→6 Pick up two 15°, one 11°, and two 15° beads and pass through all picot beads on the second rondelle.

→7 Repeat Step 6 twice. Weave to the 11° bead of the first picot **(Fig. 4)**.

→8 Pick up three 15° beads and pass through the opposite end of the 11° bead to create a reverse RAW picot.

→9 Weave to the next 11° bead and repeat Step 8 five times **(Fig. 5)**.

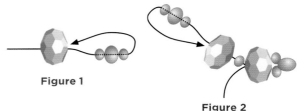

Figure 1

Figure 2

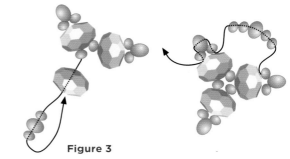

Figure 3

Figure 4

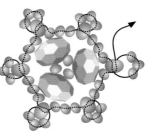

Figure 5

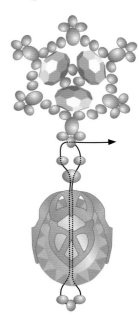

Figure 6

TIPS

→ Each quatrefoil element and its respective chain connection is about 1" (2.5 cm), and the necklace can be reduced or elongated based on this measurement.

→ Unsoldered chain links (used here) can easily be separated with chain-nose pliers.

→ Use a wooden dowel or ruler to burnish the bead cap and filigree wrap without damage to the metal (p. 13).

→ Although not necessary, you may opt to antique the silver bail of the Nouveau bead before attaching it to the necklace with liver of sulfur (p. 13).

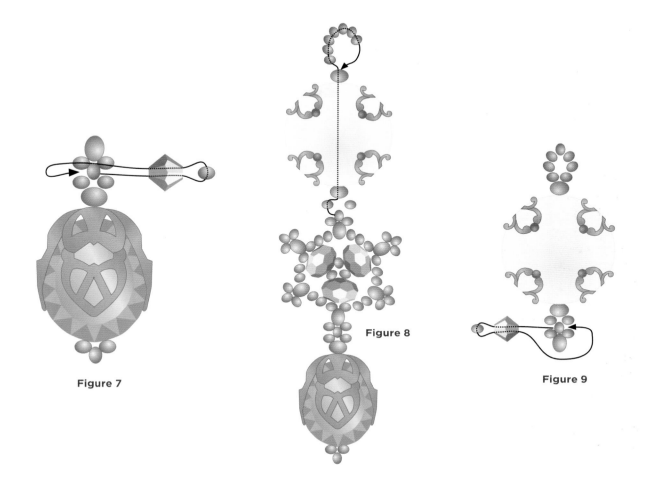

Figure 7

Figure 8

Figure 9

→**10** Weave up to the center bead of the first picot created. Pick up one 15°, one 11°, the bead cap, oval bead, and three 15° beads. Pass back through the oval, the bead cap, and the 11° bead. Pick up another 15° bead and pass back through the opposite end of the picot bead **(Fig. 6)**.

→**11** Pick up a crystal and 15° bead. Pass back through the crystal, into the opposite end of the picot bead, through the last bead of the picot sequence, and through the 11° bead **(Fig. 7)**.

→**12** Weave through all beads added in Step 10 to reinforce.

→**13** Pass under the thread from a previous pass and tie an over-hand knot. Repeat twice and trim thread.

→**14** With the 5" (13 cm) tail thread, pass through the closest 15° bead in the center into the rondelle. Weave thread to the center picot opposite of the oval bead added in Step 10.

→**15** Pick up one 15°, one 11°, coin pearl, one 11°, and seven 15° beads. Weave back through the 11° bead to create a connection loop, through the pearl, and 11° bead. Pick up another 15° bead and pass back through the opposite end of the picot bead **(Fig. 8)**.

→**16** Repeat Step 11 to add another crystal embellishment ensuring that both crystals are facing the same direction **(Fig. 9)**.

→**17** Weave through all beads added in Step 15 to reinforce.

→**18** Repeat Step 13.

→**19** Repeat Steps 2 to 18, for three additional dangle drops. Set aside for attachment later.

CREATING THE QUATREFOIL ELEMENTS

→**20** Start with 24" (61 cm) of FireLine. Pick up a pearl and eight 15° beads. Weave into the opposite end of the pearl **(Fig. 10)**.

→**21** Pick up another eight 15° beads and pass through into the opposite end of the pearl **(Fig. 11)**.

→**22** Pass CCW through the first bead on one side.

→**23** Pick up three 15° beads and pass CW through the opposite end of this first bead, creating a reverse RAW picot. Weave four beads away CCW.

→**24** Repeat Step 23 three more times **(Fig. 12)**.

→**25** Pass through into the second bead of the first picot. Pick up seven 15° beads and pass CCW through the second bead of the second picot.

→**26** Repeat Step 25 three times until an outer ring is created around the pearl center **(Fig. 13)**.

→**27** Pass through into the first bead of the first set of seven beads added in Step 25. Weave a bead into every other bead for a peyote row. There should be three high beads. Pass through the last bead, the high bead on the second picot, and the first bead on the second seven-bead sequence **(Fig. 14)**.

→**28** Repeat Step 27 three times.

→**29** Pass through the first high bead added in Step 27.

→**30** Pick up five 15° beads and pass through the last high bead of this link sequence.

→**31** Pick up one 15°, one 11°, and one 15° bead into the first high bead of the second sequence **(Fig. 15)**.

→**32** Repeat Steps 29 and 30 three times.

→**33** Weave thread to the third (center) bead of those added in Step 30. Pick up two 15°, one 11°, and two 15° beads. Weave into the opposite end of the third bead in Step 30. Reinforce this loop by weaving through all beads once more **(Fig. 16)**.

→**34** Pass under the thread from a previous pass and tie an overhand knot. Weave through two beads, repeat twice, and trim thread.

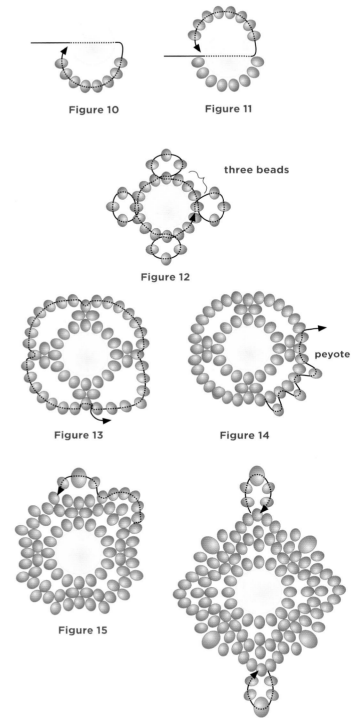

Figure 10

Figure 11

three beads

Figure 12

Figure 13

peyote

Figure 14

Figure 15

Figure 16

35 With tail thread weave to the third bead of the opposite corner of the quatrefoil following the thread path.

36 Repeat Steps 33 and 34 to create the second connection loops.

37 Repeat Steps 20 to 36, five more times to make a total of six quatrefoils.

38 Repeat Steps 20 to 32 to create another quatrefoil with no connection loops and set aside.

CENTER MEDALLION CONNECTIONS

39 With the Deco vine filigree wraps, fold in half applying stress on the joint so that the two halves split. The findings will have some sharp edges. Trim excess metal with flush cutters to soften edges.

40 On the wider end of the finding, there are two scrolls. Connect a jump ring to each of these loops. Join the two rings with another jump ring.

41 Repeat Step 40 for the two remaining findings. The wider ends will be used to connect the Nouveau bead and the necklace.

42 Using the last beaded quatrefoil element from the previous step, weave thread to one of the outside 11° beads.

43 Pick up one 15°, one 11°, and nine 15° beads. Weave through the smaller end of the finding and back through the 11° bead. Pick up another 15° bead and into the opposite end of the 11° bead on the quatrefoil. Reinforce through this connection once more by weaving through all beads added **(Fig. 17)**.

44 Weave CCW to the next 11° bead on the quatrefoil and repeat Step 43.

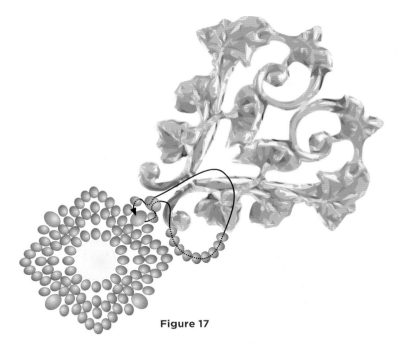

Figure 17

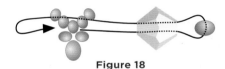

Figure 18

45 Pass under the thread from a previous pass and tie an overhand knot. Weave through two beads, repeat twice and trim thread.

46 With the tail thread, weave to the third bead on the five bead corner opposite the five-bead corner between the two findings just attached. This will create a "Y" formation.

47 Repeat Step 43 through the third bead on the quatrefoil base. Pick up a crystal and 15° bead. Pass through the crystal and into the opposite end of the third bead **(Fig. 18)**.

48 Pass under the thread from a previous pass and tie an overhand knot. Weave through two beads, repeat twice, and trim thread.

PENDANT PEYOTE-STRIP CONNECTIONS

→**49** Pick up one 11° bead and nine 15° beads. Loop into the finding in Location 1 **(Fig. 19)**. Weave back into the 11° bead and tie an overhand knot.

→**50** Pick up twenty-one 15° beads, one 11° bead, and nine 15° beads. Loop into the center finding in Location 2 **(Fig. 19)**. Weave back into the 11° bead and into the first 15° bead.

→**51** Pick up a 15° bead and weave into every other bead strung in Step 50. There should be ten high beads **(Fig. 20)**.

→**52** Pass through the connection loop and reinforce connection.

→**53** Weave to the second high bead on the outer edge. Pick up two 15°, one 11°, and two 15° beads. Weave back into the opposite end of the second high bead. Reinforce this connection loop once more and weave to the sixth high bead **(Fig. 21)**.

→**54** Pick up two 15°, one 11°, and two 15° beads. Weave back CW into the fifth high bead and into center bead joining them.

→**55** Pick up a crystal and a 15° bead. Weave back into the crystal and into the opposite end of center bead from Step 53. Pass through all beads added in Step 53 to reinforce.

→**56** Pass through peyote beads into the ninth high bead. Pick up two 15°, one 11°, and two 15° beads. Weave back into the opposite end of the ninth high bead. Reinforce this connection loop once more and weave into the connection loop to the center finding. Reinforce this connection by weaving through all beads exiting the 11° bead.

→**57** Pass under thread from a previous pass and tie an overhand knot. Weave through two beads, repeat twice, and trim thread.

→**58** With tail thread, repeat Step 57.

→**59** Repeat Steps 49 to 58 to connect Locations 3 and 4 **(Fig. 22)**.

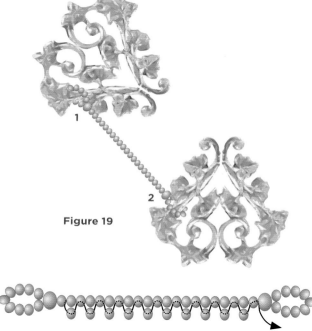

Figure 19

Figure 20

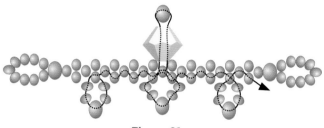

Figure 21

PUTTING IT ALL TOGETHER WITH CHAIN AND THE NOUVEAU BEAD

➔**60** Connect the Nouveau drop to the jump ring at the center.

➔**61** Separate the 17.5" (44.5 cm) of chain into the following increments: one 40-link, two 29-link, two 18-link, and six 3-link chains.

➔**62** Connect one end of the 40-link and a 29-link chain and a coin pearl dangle with a jump ring to the upper loop created on the peyote strip.

➔**63** Connect the other end of the 40-link and the other 29-link chain and a second dangle with a jump ring to the upper loop created on the second peyote loop.

➔**64** Connect one 18-link chain to the jump ring on the free end of one of the Deco vine filigrees.

➔**65** With the free end of one of the 29-link chains, connect a dangle with a jump ring to the fifteenth link of the chain added in Step 64. This location should be the third link from the end. Add a jump ring to the end of this 18-link chain and connect to one of the quatrefoil loops.

➔**66** Connect a three-link chain to each quatrefoil so that there are three quatrefoils connected on either side of the necklace with a jump ring.

➔**67** Connect the spiral hook clasp with a jump ring.

➔**68** Repeat Steps 64 to 67 for other side of necklace.

Figure 22

Double-Sided Maiden
NECKLACE

Two years after I discovered Kelly Russell's polymer clay work, we met and have since become great friends. During one of our many conversations, she mentioned that she could make double-sided cabochons for beadwork. At first I wondered why anyone would want that, but then ideas started flooding my head. This necklace design was inspired by Kelly, who shares my love of Art Nouveau.

MATERIALS
25 g matte sage iris 15° Japanese seed beads (MC)

5 g silver-lined topaz AB 15° Japanese seed beads (AC A)

1 g amethyst gold luster 15° Japanese seed beads (AC B)

1 g cranberry luster 15° Japanese seed beads (AC C)

1 g purple luster 15° Japanese seed beads (AC D)

1 g chartreuse luster 15° Japanese seed beads (AC E)

1 g sage iris 11° Japanese seed beads

33x50mm double-sided polymer clay cabochon by Kelly Russell

210 dusty rose 1x2mm seed pearls (two 16" [41 cm] strands)

4 cranberry pink 6mm glass flower beads

2 olivine 4mm Czech druk round beads

10mm shank button

6 lb FireLine

Size 12 beading needles

TOOLS
Chain-nose pliers

2 No-tangle thread bobbins

Ruler

Flush cutters

SIZE
23" (58.5 cm)

TECHNIQUES
Right-angle weave, peyote, spiral rope, branch fringe

SPIRAL NECKLACE

→**1** Start with 3 yd (2.7 m) of FireLine. From the center, wrap half of the FireLine onto the bobbin.

→**2** Pick up four 15° AC A beads and three 15° MC beads. Tie into a circle with an overhand knot. Pass through the four AC A beads again. The AC A beads will be the core beads of the spiral rope **(Fig. 1a)**.

→**3** Pick up an AC A bead, a MC bead, a seed pearl, and an MC bead **(Fig. 1b)**.

→**4** Pass through the top three core beads and the AC A bead just strung **(Fig. 1c)**.

→**5** In every sequence the thread will be woven through four core beads. As you bead the beadwork will spiral up so the beads just added will be to your left.

→**6** Pick up an AC A bead and three MC beads. Pass through the top three core beads and up the AC A bead just strung.

→**7** Repeat Steps 3 to 6 until 11" (28 cm) of the spiral strand have been created.

→**8** Repeat Steps 1 to 7 to make a second spiral strand.

ADDING THE SHANK BUTTON

→**9** Use the thread left over from making the spiral rope on the first strand. On one end, pick up an 11° bead, five MC beads, and the shank button.

→**10** Pass back through the 11° bead and through a few core beads in the rope **(Fig. 2)**. Pass under the thread of a previous pass and tie an overhand knot. Weave through into the closest outside spiral beads and reinforce with another overhand knot. Weave through the core beads and into the 11° bead.

→**11** Weave through all beads strung a second time and reinforce as in Step 10. Weave off thread into the core beads and trim thread.

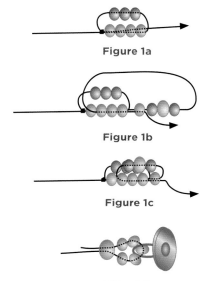

Figure 1a

Figure 1b

Figure 1c

Figure 2

TIPS

→ The spiral stitch can be beaded from either end without worrying about the orientation of the spiral beads.

→ Using a shank button in a design will allow it to be worn in reverse, which is perfect to feature the double-sided cabochon.

Figure 3a

Figure 3b

Figure 3c

MAKING THE PEYOTE LOOP

→ **12** Use the thread left over from making the spiral rope on the second strand. On one end, string one 11° bead and twenty-seven MC beads.

→ **13** Pass back through the 11° bead and test the loop over the button to make sure it fits **(Fig. 3a)**.

→ **14** Weave through a few core beads in the rope. Pass under the thread of a previous pass and tie an overhand knot. Weave through into the closest outside spiral beads and reinforce with another overhand knot. Weave through the core beads and the 11° bead.

→ **15** Weave through the 11° bead and the first MC bead. Pick up an MC bead and weave into the third MC bead of the loop. Continue picking up a MC bead and pass through every other bead. There should be thirteen high beads **(Fig. 3b)**.

→ **16** Repeat Step 14.

→ **17** Pass through the first high bead in the peyote loop. Pick up a seed pearl and weave into the next high bead of the loop. Continue picking up a seed pearl and pass through every other high bead. There should be twelve seed pearls added **(Fig. 3c)**. Pass back through the 11° bead.

→ **18** Repeat Step 14.

→ **19** Reinforce through the loop once more without adding any beads. Repeat Step 14. Weave thread into the core beads and trim thread.

BEZEL-SETTING THE CABOCHON

→**20** Start with 4 yd (3.6 m) of FireLine. From the center, wrap half of the FireLine onto the bobbin.

→**21** Pick up eight MC beads and tie into a circle with an overhand knot **(Fig. 4)**. This will create a RAW link with four sides, each consisting of two beads.

→**22** Pass through four beads CW away from the knot **(Fig. 4)**.

→**23** Pick up six MC beads and pass CCW through the last two beads from the previous link.

→**24** Pass CCW through four beads and continue making links switching thread path to CW, then CCW, etc., for 3" (8 cm).

→**25** It is time to measure the RAW strip around the cabochon to determine how many additional RAW links will be required to completely cover the cabochon side. Make sure you have an even count of RAW links so that the embellishments will be balanced. There were a total of thirty-six links made in the sample. Pull tight and visually determine how many links will be necessary to join the RAW links into a circle. Set aside the cabochon and continue making RAW links.

→**26** When you are one RAW link away from completing the circle, pick up two MC beads and pass through the two beads on the other end of the strip. Pick up two additional MC beads to return back to the last link strung **(Fig. 5)**. Weave the thread to one of the top edges of the RAW links.

→**27** Pick up three MC beads and pass through the two beads of the next RAW link, pick up one MC bead, and pass through the two beads of the next RAW link. Repeat this sequence around **(Fig. 6)**. If picots were made in every gap it would not decrease sufficiently to encapsulate the cabochon.

→**28** Wind the excess thread onto a bobbin.

→**29** Slip the cabochon into the bezel carefully to test the fit. The fit should be slightly loose as further embellishment will tighten the bezel around the cabochon in later steps. If it's too loose, you will have to step back several steps and remove up to two RAW links to remain with an even count of RAW links.

→**30** Unwind the remaining 2 yd (183 cm) of FireLine from the bobbin and repeat Step 27 on the opposite side of the RAW links. Make sure the picots line up with the picots from the first side.

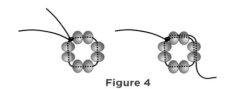

Figure 4

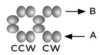

Figure 5

Figure 6

Figure 7

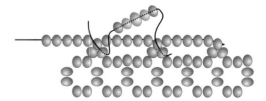

Figure 8

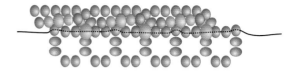

Figure 9

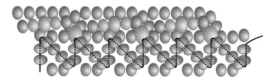

Figure 10

31 Insert cabochon into the bezel and hold carefully with the palm of your hand and thumb. It is time to cup and decrease the beading so that the cabochon will be encapsulated within the beaded bezel. Weave the thread to the closest picot, exiting the center bead (high bead).

32 Pick up five MC beads and pass through the high bead of the next picot **(Fig. 7)**.

33 Repeat Step 32 around the bezel for all high beads. Reinforce through all beads strung once more. Pass under the thread from a previous pass and tie an overhand knot.

34 Repeat Steps 32 and 33 for the other side of the bezel.

EMBELLISHING THE BEZEL BASE

35 Pass through the existing thread path until the thread exits from the second or center bead of the picot. Pass under the thread from a previous pass and make an overhand knot. Embellishments will be stitched diagonally in the largest exposed section between the picots.

36 Weave through until exiting the third bead of the picot. Pick up an AC A bead, a MC bead, a seed pearl, an MC bead and an AC A bead. Pass through the high bead of the next picot sequence and down into the adjoining third bead of the picot **(Fig. 8)**.

37 Repeat Step 36 around the bezel.

38 There are still some gaps left at the corners of the RAW links. Weave the thread into the top side of the RAW links. Pick up an 11° bead and weave it in the gap between links. Repeat around **(Fig. 9)**.

39 Repeat Steps 36 to 38 on the other side of the bezel.

40 The RAW links themselves are still exposed with some of the polymer clay cabochon showing through. To cover the links, pick up four MC beads and weave diagonally to the opposite side of the RAW link. Pass through the opposite diagonal corner with the needle facing the same direction as the original thread path through two beads. Continue adding embellishments in this sequence for the remaining links **(Fig. 10)**.

CONNECTING SPIRAL ROPES TO THE CABOCHON

Remember the diagonal embellishments added to the RAW links on the cabochon bezel in the previous section, Step 40? These embellishments will be guides to attach the spiral ropes to the cabochon. You want even distribution so that the cabochon will lay properly. For balance, make sure you like the way the pendant hangs before you secure the thread on the first connection. Refer to Fig. 11 for suggested locations for these connections.

→**41** Pick up one 11° bead and three MC beads. Pass through the RAW embellishment link you have selected.

→**42** Pick up three MC beads and pass back through the 11° bead **(Fig. 11)**.

→**43** Weave back through a few core beads in the rope. Pass under the thread of a previous pass and tie an overhand knot. Weave through into the closest outside spiral beads and reinforce with another overhand knot. Weave through the core beads down to the 11° bead.

→**44** Weave through all beads strung a second time and reinforce as in Step 43. Weave into the core beads and trim thread.

→**45** Repeat Steps 41 to 44 on other side to connect to Location 2.

EMBELLISHING WITH VINES AND FLOWERS

Refer to **Fig. 12a** for the approximate location where the branch fringes should be added. The fringe will range from a six to fifteen vine bead start, depending on how long you want your fringe to hang. Some of the fringe will be tacked onto the bezel base, so they can be a bit longer.

→**46** Use 1 yd (91.5 cm) of FireLine and weave the new thread exiting Region 1. Tie an overhand knot over a previous thread path, leaving an 8" (20.5 cm) tail.

→**47** Using a random mix of green 15° beads (MC and AC E), string fifteen beads. The branches will end with picots in three shades of flower colors (15° bead mix of AC B, C, and D). Pick up a random set of three flower beads and pass back through three beads in the vine.

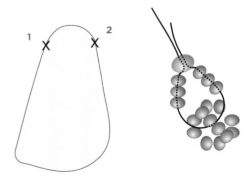

Figure 11

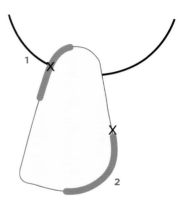

Figure 12a

Figure 12b

→**48** Pick up three vine beads and three flower beads. Pass back through the three vine beads added and up three beads on the main vine. Continue branching off until reaching the top of the main vine **(Fig. 12b)**.

→**49** You may have your fringes just hang freely, but I like to tack a few of them down randomly as if the vines were winding around the bezel edge. To do this, weave through a few bezel beads and exit out from where you'd like to tack the fringe down. String through the respective vine bead and then back into the closest bezel bead.

→**50** Move the thread to a lower location in Region 1 and make another fringe. The fringes should get shorter and shorter as you move lower on the bezel edge. This will create a tiered effect. Add as many fringes as you'd like, then weave thread into the cabochon bezel and tie off.

→**51** With the tail end of the thread, weave the thread exiting where you'd like to add the flower and druk bead embellishments. On **Fig. 12a**, the "X" marks approximate locations where the glass flowers were added.

→**52** Pick up a flower bead, an AC B bead, and pass back through the flower bead. Tack this embellishment down by weaving into the closest bezel bead below. Weave a few beads away on the bezel.

→**53** Repeat Step 53 with a druk bead and an AC B bead.

→**54** Repeat Step 53 to add a second flower bead.

→**55** Weave through several bezel beads, pass under the thread from a previous pass, and tie an overhand knot. Weave through several bezel beads and trim thread.

→**56** Repeat Steps 47 to 56 to embellish Region 2.

Medici Rhinestone
NECKLACE

One of my favorite pastimes is perusing museum books and auction catalogs to read up on the history of jewelry. Many of my beadwork designs are inspired by these images that become embedded in my mind. Renaissance paintings of aristocratic ladies bedecked with elaborate jewels created by the finest craftsman were an inspiration for this design. During that period (fourteenth to fifteenth centuries), jeweled medallion necklaces were often decorated with rubies, sapphires, emeralds, and diamonds.

MATERIALS
20 g silver-lined topaz cranberry AB

10 g cranberry 15° Japanese seed beads (AC)

6 g matte cranberry 11° Japanese seed beads

9 rose 14mm Swarovski 4671 Square Octagonal Vintage Rhinestones

8 champagne luster 9x10mm oval faceted glass beads

4 champagne luster 3mm Czech firepolished beads

4 champagne 6mm freshwater pearls

16 gold-plated 6mm bead caps with inset

6 lb FireLine

Size 12 beading needles

TOOLS
Chain-nose pliers

Round-nose pliers

Flush cutters

No-tangle thread bobbin

SIZE
20" (51 cm)

TECHNIQUES
Circular peyote, ladder stitch, netting, picot

CREATING LINKS

➜1 Using 1 yd (91.5 cm) of thread, pick up one 11° bead and twenty-seven MC 15° beads. Pass back through the 11° bead **(Fig. 1)**.

➜2 Pick up one bead cap, the oval bead, one bead cap, one 11° bead, and twenty-seven 15° MC beads. Pass back through the 11° bead, through the oval, and out to the opposite 11° bead.

➜3 Pass through the first 15° bead. Pick up a 15° MC, skip a bead on the base loop, and pass through the next bead in the loop. Continue this step around the loop until there are thirteen 15° high beads added **(Fig. 2)**.

➜4 Pass through the last 15° bead, the 11° bead, through the oval bead and out to the other side's 11° bead.

➜5 Repeat Steps 3 and 4.

➜6 Pass through the first high bead of the third row, pick up one 11° bead, and pass through the next high bead. Continue around the loop. There should be twelve 11° high beads added **(Fig. 3)**.

➜7 Pass through the last 15° bead, the 11° bead, through the oval, and out to the opposite 11° bead.

➜8 Repeat Steps 6 and 7.

➜9 Weave to the sixth high bead and leave remaining thread for connections later.

TIP

➜ Stick with 14mm rhinestones. Although the shapes are similar between the vintage Swarovski and German 4671 rhinestones, Swarovski crystal rhinestones will have more sparkle than vintage German glass rhinestones.

➜10 Weave tail thread through the outside peyote row. Pass under the thread of a previous pass and tie an overhand knot. Repeat twice and trim tail thread.

➜11 Repeat Steps 1 to 10 to make seven additional links.

BEZELED RHINESTONES

➜12 Using 1 yd (91.5 cm) of thread, pick up twenty 15° AC A seed beads, and tie into a ring with an overhand knot. Pass through two beads and tie another knot. Repeat once more and trim tail thread **(Fig. 4)**.

➜13 Pass through two beads. Pick up a 15° bead, skip a bead in the ring, and pass through the next bead in the ring. Continue adding beads around the ring and step up on last stitch by passing through the first bead added in this row. This creates three rows of circular peyote. There should be ten high beads **(Fig. 5)**.

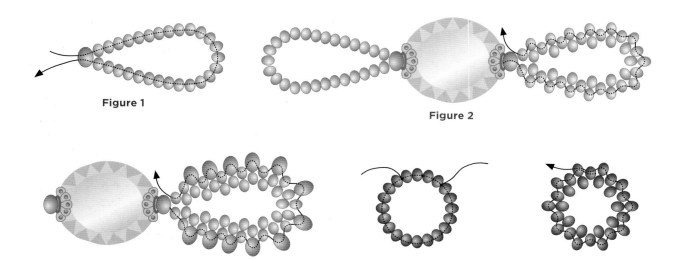

Figure 1

Figure 2

Figure 3

Figure 4

Figure 5

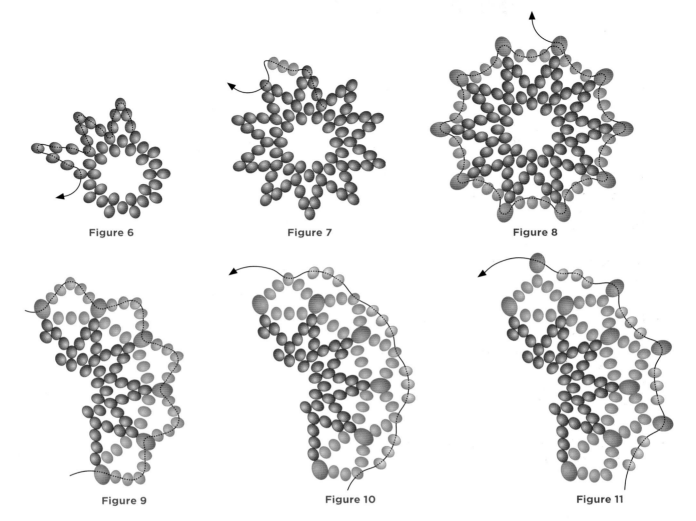

Figure 6

Figure 7

Figure 8

Figure 9

Figure 10

Figure 11

→**14** Pick up five beads and pass through every high bead. This creates a picot. Step up on last stitch by weaving into the top bead of the first picot **(Fig. 6)**.

→**15** Switch to the 15° main color (MC) bead. Pick up three 15° beads and weave into the high bead of the second picot. Repeat nine times to connect all remaining picots **(Fig. 7)**.

→**16** Pass through the first set of three beads added in Step 15. Treat the three beads as one element. Weave one 11° bead in between each of the three beads. There should be ten 11° beads added **(Fig. 8)**.

→**17** Weave to the next 11° bead and pick up five MC 15° beads to create a picot. Repeat nine times. Weave into the first 11° bead and step up into the top (third) picot bead **(Fig. 9)**.

→**18** Insert the rhinestone into the bezel. Pick up three 15° beads and weave into the third bead of the second picot created in Step 17. Repeat nine times **(Fig. 10)**.

→**19** Switch to the 11° bead. Tighten the bezel by adding one 11° bead in between the three beads added in Step 18. Treat the 3 beads as one element. Pass through all beads in the last two rows once more to tighten. With the proper tension, the bezel will appear scalloped **(Fig. 11)**.

→**20** Weave down into the back of beadwork. Pass thread under a previous pass and tie a knot. Repeat twice and trim thread.

→**21** Repeat Steps 12 to 20 for seven additional rhinestones.

RHINESTONE MEDALLION

→**22** Start with 3 yd (2.9 m) of FireLine. From the center, wrap half of the Fireline onto the bobbin. This method will reduce the necessity to add thread.

→**23** Repeat Steps 12 to 20 to bezel the last rhinestone. Weave to the first 11° row from Step 16.

→**24** Pick up a 15° MC bead, one pearl, and one 15° MC bead. Pass back through the pearl and pick up one 15° MC bead. Pass through the next 11° bead.

→**25** Skip the next 11° bead and pass through the 11° bead two beads away. Follow the thread path of previous beading on the bezel.

→**26** Pick up one pearl and one 15° MC bead. Pass back through the pearl and through the opposite end of the 11° bead.

→**27** Repeat Steps 25 and 26 to add the last two pearls **(Fig. 12)**.

→**28** Weave to the 11° bead without a pearl embellishment. Pick up twenty-seven 15° MC beads and weave into the next free 11° bead **(Fig. 13)**.

→**29** Repeat Step 28 three more times to connect the remaining free 11° beads on the rhinestone bezel.

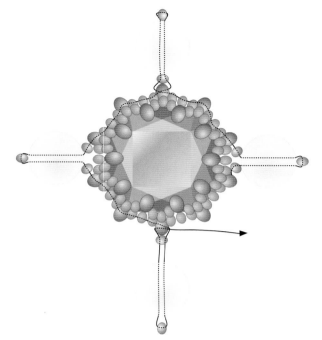

Figure 12

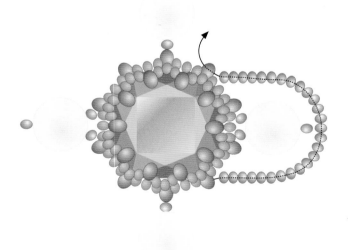

Figure 13

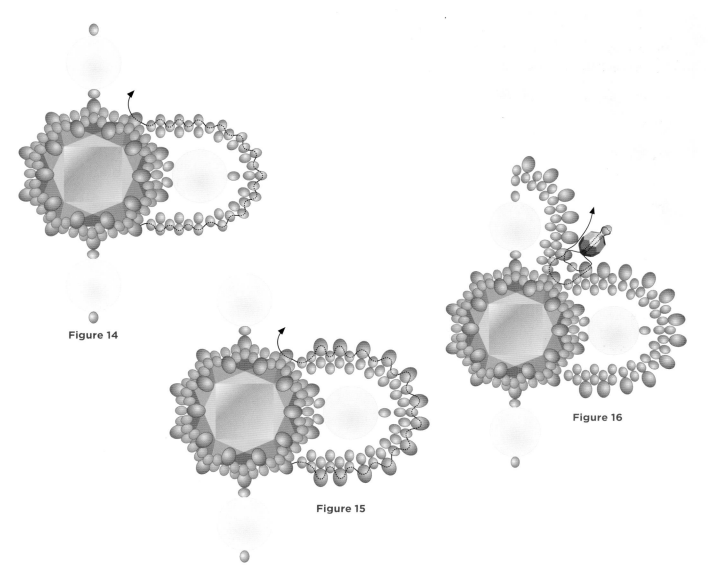

Figure 14

Figure 15

Figure 16

→**30** Pass through the first 11° bead in Step 28 and the first 15° MC bead. Weave a 15° MC bead into every other bead for a peyote row. There should be thirteen high beads. Pass through the last 15° MC bead and into the next 11° bead **(Fig. 14)**.

→**31** Repeat Step 30 for the other loops.

→**32** Pass through the first 11° bead in Step 28, the 15° MC bead, and into the first 15° MC bead of the third row. Weave one 11° bead into every high bead. There should be twelve high

beads. Weave through the 15° MC bead and into the next 11° bead **(Fig. 15)**.

→**33** Repeat Step 32 for the other loops.

→**34** Weave to the first 11° bead of the adjoining ring added in Step 32. Pick up a firepolished and one 15° MC bead. Weave back through the firepolished and into the adjoining 11° bead of the adjacent loop. Pick up one 15° MC bead and then weave up the 11° bead **(Fig. 16)**.

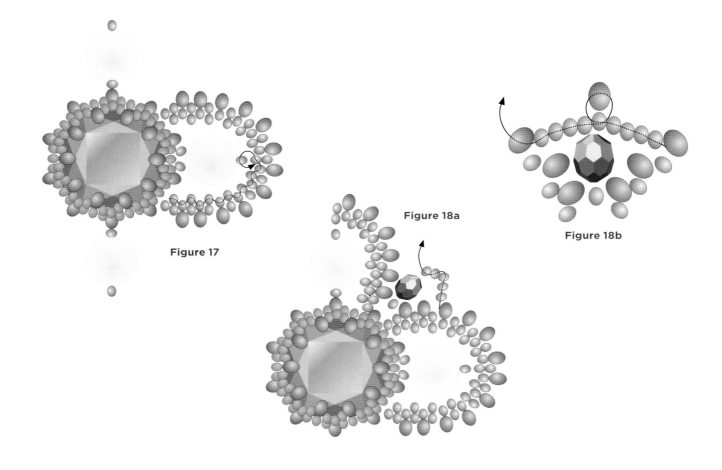

Figure 17

Figure 18a

Figure 18b

→35 Weave through the beadwork until reaching the seventh inner high 15° bead. Ladder-stitch to the 15° MC bead on the pearl twice and weave back into the loop **(Fig. 17)**.

→36 Repeat Steps 34 and 35 three more times.

→37 Weave to the tenth 11° bead on the last row of loop. Pick up four 15° beads and pass through the 15° bead on the firepolished. Pick up one 11° bead and ladder stitch to the 15° bead on the firepolished twice. Pick up four 15° beads and pass through the third 11° bead of the next loop **(Figs. 18a and 18b)**.

→38 Repeat Step 36 for the other loops.

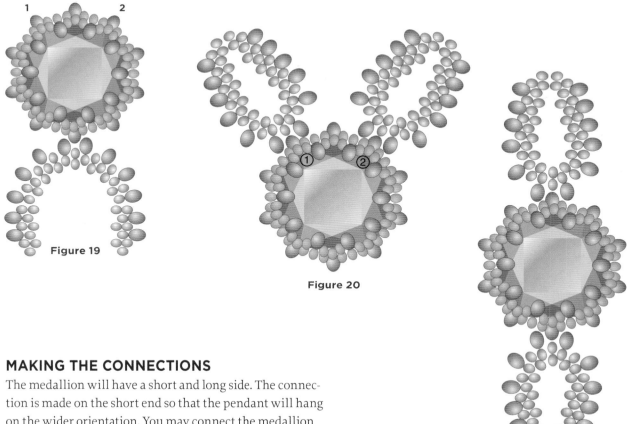

Figure 19

Figure 20

Figure 21

MAKING THE CONNECTIONS

The medallion will have a short and long side. The connection is made on the short end so that the pendant will hang on the wider orientation. You may connect the medallion in any orientation using the same steps. Each bezel has an 11° bead row to aid in supporting the bezel and allow the components to be connected more easily. This row will be used to make peyote "zip" stitches for connecting the bezels to the links.

→**39** From the medallion, weave the thread to exit from the sixth 11° bead of the loop on the shortest side. This location should be opposite of the pearl connection. Weave into a 11° bead on the rhinestone bezel and then into the next 11° bead on the medallion loop. Pass under the thread from a previous pass and tie a knot. Weave back to the connection to reinforce. Repeat once more **(Fig. 19)**.

→**40** Weave through the rhinestone bezel four 11° beads CCW from this connection (Location 1 on **Fig. 19)**. Pass through the sixth bead of the loop. Make connections on the free

side of the loop without the extraneous working thread. Pass under the thread from a previous pass and tie an overhand knot. Weave back through beads and secure connection to the seventh bead on the loop. Reinforce once more **(Fig. 20)**.

→**41** Weave two beads CW from this connection (Location 2 on **Fig. 19)**. Repeat Step 39 with another loop.

→**42** Repeat connecting the links and rhinestones as in Step 39 but with the connections made at the 12 o'clock and 6 o'clock 11° bead locations on the rhinestone bezel. There should be four 11° beads in between each connection **(Fig. 21)**.

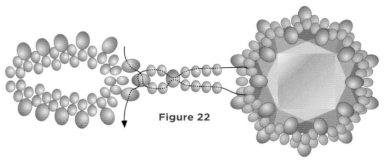

Figure 22

BUTTON LOOP

→**43** Using 1 yd (91.5 cm) of thread, pick up fifty 15° MC beads and join into a ring with an overhand knot. Pass through two beads and knot again. Repeat once more and trim tail thread.

→**44** Pick up a 15° bead and pass through every other bead of the ring. Step up on last stitch by weaving into the first bead added in this row. This creates three rows of circular peyote.

→**45** Pick up one 11° bead and pass through each high bead around. Step up on last stitch by passing through the first bead added in this row.

→**46** Pass under thread from a previous pass and tie a knot. Weave through two beads and knot again. Repeat twice and trim thread.

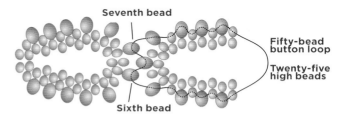

Seventh bead

Fifty-bead button loop

Twenty-five high beads

Sixth bead

Figure 23

CONNECTING THE BUTTON RHINESTONE

→**47** The last bezel rivoli is used for the button closure. Weave the thread to exit from the sixth 11° bead on the link. Pick up one 11° bead and pass through the seventh 11° bead on the link.

→**48** Pick up two 15° MC beads, one 11° bead, and four 15° MC beads. Pass through a low bead on the second row of beading on the rhinestone bezel. Pass through the adjacent high bead on the first row and back to the respective adjoining low bead on the second row.

→**49** Pick up four 15° MC beads and weave back into the 11° bead. Pick up two 15° MC beads and weave into the opposite end of the sixth bead on the link. Reinforce once more through all beads added **(Fig. 22)**.

→**50** Weave through the outside peyote row on the link. Pass under the thread of a previous pass and tie an overhand knot. Repeat twice and trim thread.

CONNECTING THE BUTTON LOOP

→**51** Weave the thread to exit from the sixth 11° bead on the link. Pass through one of the 11° beads on the button loop and through the seventh 11° bead on the link **(Fig. 23)**.

→**52** Pass under the thread from a previous pass and tie an overhand knot. Turn beadwork and reinforce the link just connected twice. Pass through two beads and knot. Repeat twice and trim thread.

USING ALTERNATE SWAROVSKI RIVOLIS

The Swarovski rhinestones used in this project are vintage and therefore may not be easy to find. You can substitute 1122 Swarovski rivolis, which are bezel-set with the same combination of stitches as the vintage 4671 rhinestones, but instead of a five-bead picot in Step 14, the 1122 will only need a three-bead picot sequence. Step 19 will switch from a size 11° to a 15° bead to lock the smaller rivoli in place.

Deco Collar
WITH GEMSTONE DROPS

Following the Art Nouveau era, Art Deco became the trend from 1920 to 1939, reaching peak popularity during the Roaring Twenties. The Art Deco style contrasted the stylized and flowing lines of its predecessor with more structural, linear motifs. This collar embodies the "transition" of Art Nouveau to Art Deco. The deco motif is brought to life by the ornate clasp that serves as both the closure and a decorative component. The clasp is adorned with five gemstone drops, which together make up the tiered pendant. The collar is terminated with bead caps encrusted with cubic zirconias, a finishing touch that lends a classy exuberance to the piece.

MATERIALS

3 g each of matte rose gold, cranberry bronze, and matte cabernet 11° Japanese triangle beads

6 g fuchsia crystal-lined 15° Japanese seed beads

1 g gold 13° charlottes

2 lt. rose satin 4mm Swarovski bicone beads

5 ametrine gemstone drops in graduated formation 8x13mm to 8x15mm

15" (38.5 cm) of clear 2mm rubber cord

2 vermeil 12mm cubic zirconia bead caps

1 vermeil 19x7 mm cubic zircon floral Deco clasp

6" (15.5 cm) of gold-filled 24-gauge wire

6 lb FireLine

Size 12 beading needles

TOOLS

Chain-nose pliers

Round-nose pliers

Flush cutters

Ruler

SIZE

18" (46 cm) (measured end to end)

TECHNIQUES

Odd-count tubular peyote, fringe

ODD-COUNT TUBULAR PEYOTE COLLAR

Tubular peyote stitch naturally spirals when there is
an odd count, so there is no need to step up at the end of
each row.

→1 Start with 1.5 yd (1.4 m) of FireLine. Leave a 12" (30.5 cm) tail
for weaving the bead cap later. Pick up two 15° beads and one
triangle bead, five times. Tie into a circle with an overhand
knot. Pass through the first triangle and two 15° beads.

→2 Pick up one triangle and two 15° beads and pass through
the first 15° bead of the next sequence **(Fig. 1)**.

→3 Repeat Step 2 with the first triangle color for a total of 5"
(13 cm).

→4 The transition to the second triangle color should be
gradual for better blending. To achieve this, two rows of
beading or about ten sequences are beaded before moving
to the second triangle color. Achieving this is random and
visual but the following are some suggestions: 1st color,
2nd color, 1st color, 2nd color, 2nd color, 1st color, 2nd color,
1st color, 1st color, and 2nd color. Remember that there are
two 15° beads following each triangle.

→5 Repeat Step 2 with second color triangle for another 5"
(13 cm).

→6 Repeat Step 4 to transition to third color triangle.

→7 Repeat Step 2 with third color triangle for the last 5" (13 cm).

TIPS

→ I prefer Toho triangles because they have large holes and sharp
edges that fit together symmetrically as they are beaded. For a
different look, you can easily substitute Miyuki triangles (which
have rounded edges) or other beads of a similar size.

→ Add new thread through the spiral beads leaving a 5" (13 cm) tail
thread. Weave tail thread into beadwork with several half hitch or
overhand knots in between weaving through several beads.

→ A smaller or larger tube can be created by adding or reducing
the start by odd-count increments. The bead-cap used in this
project perfectly fits a five-increment start.

→ Any stiff cord (which adds structure) up to 4mm can be incor-
porated. Select cord color based on bead colors.

→8 The last row of beading tapers the tube to mirror the start side.
Continue beading the last row consisting of five sequences by
only using one triangle and one 15° bead **(Fig. 2)**.

→9 Pick up two 15° beads, one triangle, and two 15° beads and
pass through the triangle on the opposite side of the tube.
Weave CCW to the next triangle sequence **(Fig. 3)**.

→10 Pick up two 15° beads and pass through the center triangle
bead. Pick up another two 15° beads and pass through the
triangle on the opposite side of the tube **(Fig. 4)**.

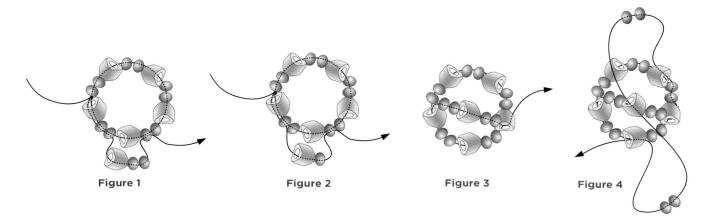

Figure 1   Figure 2   Figure 3   Figure 4

Figure 5

Figure 6

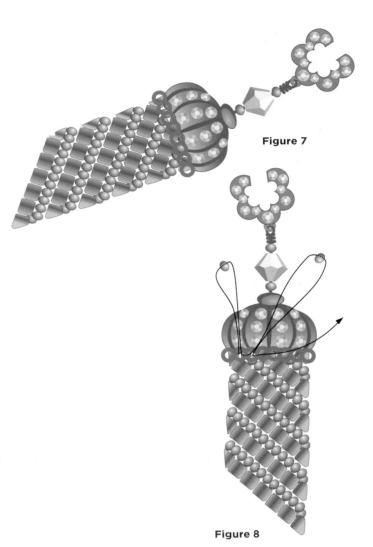

Figure 7

Figure 8

→ **11** Weave through two 15° beads from the spiral and pass under the thread from a previous pass and tie an overhand knot. Reserve the excess thread to attach the bead cap later **(Fig. 5)**.

→ **12** With 3" (8 cm) of wire, create a wrapped loop around the triangle bead from Step 9 **(Fig. 6)**.

→ **13** Pass the wire through a bead cap. Pick up a charlotte, a crystal, and a charlotte. Create another wrapped loop, including one side of the clasp **(Fig. 7)**.

→ **14** There are nine holes on the bead cap, and these will serve to lock the bead cap to the tube. With the thread from Step 11, string through adjacent triangle beads or spiral beads to the closest hole on the bead cap. It will be easier to weave through the hole if you position your needle at a diagonal. Pick up a 15° bead and pass back through the same hole into the tube **(Fig. 8)**.

→ **15** Weave carefully down several beads in the beadwork and back up to the next hole, CCW. Repeat Step 14 for the remaining eight holes. You are tacking down to the spiral at each interval to secure the bead cap.

→ **16** Weave thread through the spiral beads. Pass under thread from a previous pass and tie a knot. Weave through several more spiral beads, repeat twice, and trim thread.

→ **17** On the other open end, string the rubber cord through the hollow tube.

→ **18** Repeat Steps 9 to 16 to attach the other bead cap to the clasp.

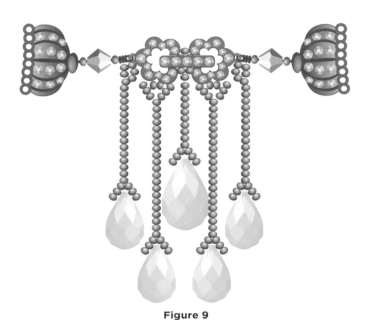

Figure 9

ADDING THE EMBELLISHMENT DROPS

Refer to **Fig. 9** for the orientation of each branch.

19 With 24" (61 cm) of FireLine, pick up three 15° beads and pass through one of the wrapped loops.

20 Pick up three 15° beads and pass through the first bead from Step 19. Leaving a 5" (13 cm) tail thread, tie the tail thread to the working thread with an overhand knot.

21 Alternate randomly between the 15° beads and the charlottes, pick up a total of fifteen beads for the fringe stem.

22 Pick up three 15° beads, a gemstone drop, and three 15° beads. Pass back through the last bead of the fringe stem.

23 Pass under the thread from a previous pass and tie an overhand knot. Weave through three beads and tie another knot.

24 Weave through all beads in the connection loop to reinforce and down fringe stem.

25 Repeat Step 23 and trim thread.

26 With the tail thread, weave through all beads on the fringe stem and all beads connecting the gemstone drop to reinforce.

27 Repeat Step 23 and trim thread.

28 Repeat Steps 19 to 27 for the fringe stem on other wrapped loop.

29 There are two loops on the bottom of each side of the clasp. These loops are used for the second and fourth fringes.

30 Pick up four 15° beads and pass through one of these loops facing the center, leaving a 5" (13 cm) tail thread.

31 Pick up two 15° beads and pass through the second loop.

32 Pick up three 15° beads and weave into the first bead strung in Step 30.

33 Tie the tail thread to the working thread with an overhand knot.

34 Alternate randomly between the 15° beads and the charlottes, pick up a total of twenty beads for the fringe stem.

35 Repeat Steps 22 to 27.

36 Repeat Steps 30 to 35 for the fourth fringe stem.

37 The last fringe is created on the back of the clasp closure itself.

38 Pick up eight 15° beads, loop over the center of the bar of the clasp closure. Pass through the first bead strung and tie the tail thread to the working thread with an overhand knot. Leave a 5" (13 cm) tail thread.

39 Alternate randomly between the 15° beads and the charlottes, pick up a total of ten beads for the last fringe stem.

40 Repeat Steps 22 to 27.

Black Lace
LARIAT

This design is inspired by Victorian lacework and Whitby jet mourning necklaces, en vogue during Queen Victoria's reign (1837 to 1901). I decided to design with Czech charlottes in a monochromatic palette because black was the traditional color used for these necklaces. The faceted cuts on the charlottes catch the light at every angle so, although the piece is entirely black, the design elements are not lost in the beadwork.

MATERIALS
3 hanks black 13° Czech charlottes

1 hank black 11° Czech charlottes

1 g black 11° Japanese triangle beads

391 black 2 to 3mm Czech firepolished beads

42 black 3x10mm Czech dagger beads

4 black 8x12mm oval faceted beads

4 black 6x10mm teardrop faceted beads

Black Silamide thread

Size 12 beading needles

Size 13 beading needles

TOOLS
Chain-nose pliers

Beeswax

SIZE
47.25" (120.5 cm)

TECHNIQUE
Circular and flat odd-count peyote, brick-stitch picot, fringe

FIRST FLOWER MEDALLION

→1 With 1 yd (91.5 cm) of thread, string twenty 13° beads and tie into a circle with an overhand knot. Pass through two beads to get away from the knot **(Fig. 1)**.

→2 Pick up a 13° bead and pass through every other bead of the ring. Step up on last stitch by passing through the first bead added in this row. This creates three rows of circular peyote **(Fig. 2)**.

→3 Weave one 11° bead into every 13° bead from Step 2 for the fourth row. Step up on last stitch by passing through the first bead added in this row **(Fig. 3)**.

→4 Pick up a firepolished and three 13° beads. Pass back through the firepolished and into the next 11° bead. Repeat nine times **(Fig. 4)**.

→5 Weave into the top (second) picot bead above the first fire-polished. Pick up five 13° beads and pass through the next high bead of the second picot. Repeat nine times until all picots are connected in a ring **(Fig. 5)**.

→6 Weave to the third bead of the first five beads added in Step 4. Pick up three 13° beads and pass through the opposite end of the bead just exited, creating a RAW link or reverse picot. Repeat nine times **(Fig. 6)**.

→7 Weave tail thread by passing under the thread of a previous pass and tie an overhand knot. Repeat twice and then trim thread. Leave working thread untrimmed for connections later and set aside medallion.

REMAINING FLOWER MEDALLIONS

→8 Repeat Steps 1 to 5. The picots for the second and subsequent flower medallions share four picots with two neighboring medallions.

→9 Weave thread to the third bead of the five beads added in Step 5. Pick up one 13° bead and pass through the top bead of one of the picots on the first medallion. Pick up one 13° bead and pass back through the opposite end of the third bead to create a reverse picot.

→10 Repeat Step 9 once more to connect another picot to the first medallion **(Fig. 7)**.

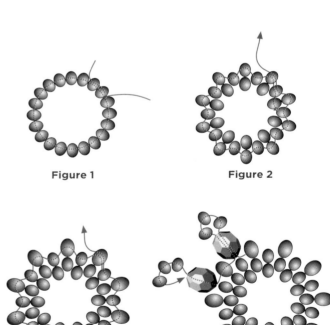

Figure 1   Figure 2

Figure 3   Figure 4

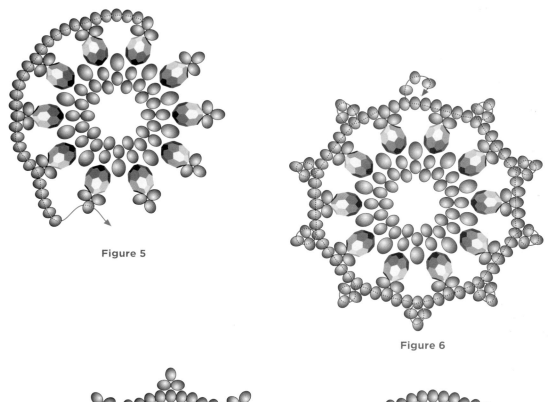

Figure 5

Figure 6

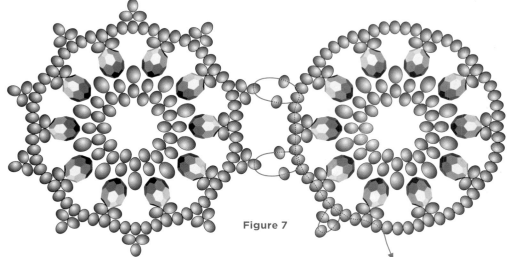

Figure 7

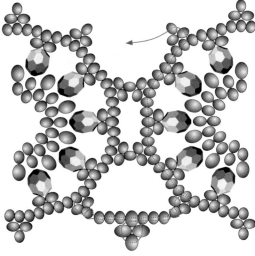

Figure 8

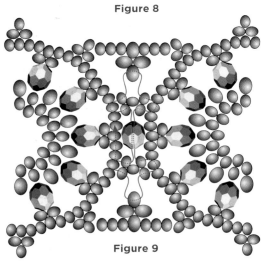

Figure 9

Figure 10

→**11** Weave to the third bead of the next group of five beads added in the last round. Pick up three 13° beads and make a reverse picot as in Step 6. Continue around, adding a total of seven new picots.

→**12** Circle around and weave back to the top bead of the last picot added. Pick up three 13°, one 11°, and three 13° beads. Weave into the complementary top picot bead of the first medallion.

→**13** Circle around this picot and weave back into the three 13° beads and 11° bead added in Step 12. Pick up three 11° beads and weave into the opposite end of the 11° bead from Step 12 to create a reverse picot. Weave through the last three 13° beads **(Fig. 8)**.

→**14** Weave thread to the other end of medallion following the thread path and repeat Steps 12 and 13 to join complementary picots.

→**15** Weave to the first picot bead of the adjoining picots at the center (created in Steps 9 and 10). Weave into the top 11° picot bead added in Step 13 and then into the complementary first picot bead on the second medallion **(Fig. 9)**.

→**16** Circle around this picot and exit into the third picot bead. String a firepolished and weave into the opposite first bead of the adjoining picot.

→**17** Circle around this picot and exit into the third picot bead. Weave into the top 11° picot bead added in Step 14 and then into the complementary third picot bead on the first medallion.

→**18** Circle around this picot and exit into the first bead of this picot. Weave down into the firepolished added in Step 16 and weave into the opposite third bead of the adjoining picot **(Fig. 10)**.

→**19** Weave towards the center of the medallion. Pass under the thread from a previous pass and tie an overhand knot. Repeat twice and trim thread.

→**20** Weave tail thread by passing under the thread from a previous pass and tie an overhand knot. Repeat twice and then trim thread.

→**21** Two medallions have been joined. All subsequent medallions will be added in this manner. Repeat Steps 8 to 20 for twenty-eight additional flower medallions. If you desire a shorter lariat, reduce the number of flower medallions, which are each about 1" (2.5 cm).

LARIAT RINGLETS

Refer to the diagram **(Fig. 11)** for the suggested sequence of connections. Six rings are required for each side of the lariat. The second side of the lariat is beaded in reverse order to the first to add some visual contrast, but you can make yours the same if you wish.

→**22** Pick up twenty 13° beads and tie into a circle with an overhand knot. Pass through one bead to get away from the knot.

→**23** Pick up one 13° bead and pass through every other bead on the ring. Step up on last stitch by passing through the first bead added in this row. This creates three rows of circular peyote.

→**24** Weave one 11° bead into every 13° bead from Step 2 for the fourth row. Step up on last stitch by passing through the first bead added in this row.

→**25** Weave a firepolished into an 11° bead from Step 24. Repeat seven times.

→**26** The last two stitches will join the ringlet to the end medallions through two shared center picots. Weave into the high bead of the picot of the last medallion.

→**27** Pick up one 13° bead and weave into the next 11° bead of the ringlet. Pick up another 13° bead and pass through the top picot bead of the adjoining picot on the medallion. Weave into the last 11° bead on the ringlet and into the next firepolished **(Fig. 12)**.

→**28** Pass under the thread from a previous pass and tie an overhand knot. Weave back through connection to reinforce once more.

→**29** Weave through the adjoining firepolished on the ringlet. Pass under the thread from a previous pass and tie an overhand knot. Repeat twice and trim thread.

→**30** Start a second ring as in Steps 22 to 25.

→**31** The last two stitches will join the second ringlet to the first through two shared firepolished beads. Weave into the firepolished bead of the first ringlet (these connections are the two center firepolished beads opposite of the connections made to the flower medallion). Weave into the 11° bead and into the next firepolished bead on the first ringlet. Weave into the last 11° bead of the second ringlet and into its adjoining firepolished bead.

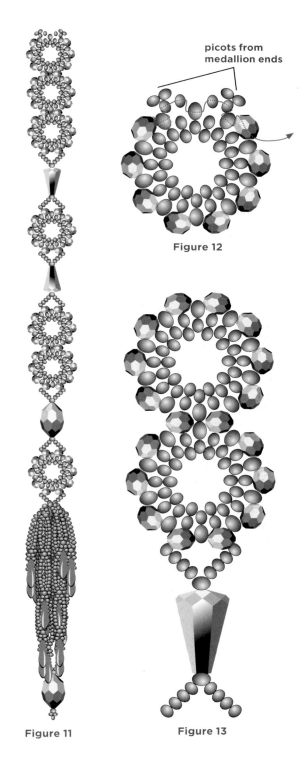

Figure 11

picots from medallion ends

Figure 12

Figure 13

Figure 14

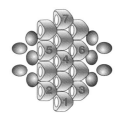

Figure 15   **Figure 16**

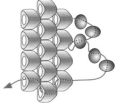

Figure 17

→**32** Repeat Steps 28 and 29.

→**33** Repeat Steps 22 to 25, 31, and 28 to 29 for third ringlet.

→**34** Repeat Steps 22 to 25 to make a regular ringlet with ten fire-polished instead of eight. Weave into the next firepolished.

→**35** Pick up four 13°, one 11°, a teardrop, one 11°, and four 13° beads. Weave into the adjoining center pair of firepolished beads created on the third ringlet following the peyote thread path.

→**36** Pick up four 13° beads. Pass back through the 11° bead, the teardrop, and the 11° bead. Pick up four 13° beads and pass through the opposite end of the firepolished one bead away from the previous **(Fig. 13)**.

→**37** Reinforce connection by weaving through all beads added in Steps 35 and 36 once more.

→**38** Weave into the adjoining firepolished. Pass under the thread from a previous pass and tie an overhand knot. Weave through another firepolished and into the center of the ringlet and then trim thread.

→**39** Repeat Steps 22 to 25 to make a regular ringlet with ten firepolished instead of eight. Weave into the next firepolished. Repeat Steps 35 to 38 to join another drop bead but in reverse orientation.

→**40** Repeat Steps 22 to 25, and 28 and 29 to complete the sixth ringlet.

→**41** Repeat Steps 22 to 25 to make a regular ringlet with ten firepolished instead of eight. Weave into the next firepolished. Repeat Steps 34 to 38 to join the oval bead to the sixth ringlet.

→**42** Repeat Steps 22 to 41 for the other side of lariat but in reverse orientation.

MAKING THE TASSELS

The tassel fringe is built on top of a flat strip of odd-count peyote. There are nine rows of odd-count peyote.

43 With 24" (61 cm) of thread, pick up four triangle beads and pass back through the second bead, opposite the thread path.

44 Pick up one triangle and pass back through the first bead following the thread path. Pull tight to align the beads.

45 Weave through the second, fourth, and third bead. Pick up one triangle and pass through the first bead. Continue odd-count peyote and turning thread path as shown in **Fig. 14**. Nine rows are required to add the tassel fringe.

46 Weave thread to the edge to add two brick-stitch picots on the outer edge to hide threads. Pick up three beads and pass under the edge thread on top of the second bead and pass back through the last bead strung. Pick up two beads and pass through the fourth edge bead and into the beadwork to the opposite edge. Repeat, adding brick-stitch picots on second edge **(Fig. 15)**.

47 Weave thread to the center end bead on the strip to attach to the last ringlet. Pick up four 13° beads and weave into the adjoining center pair of firepolished on the sixth ringlet following the peyote thread path.

48 Pick up four 13° beads and pass back through the triangle bead.

49 Reinforce connection by weaving through all beads added in Steps 47 and 48 once more **(Fig. 16)**.

50 Weave thread into the sixth ringlet. Pass under the thread from a previous pass and tie an overhand knot. Repeat twice and trim thread.

51 Use a new 1.5 yd (1.3 m) length of thread for the tassels. Refer to **Fig. 17** for the suggested tassel locations. Add thread through the edges by passing under the thread of the outside picots and tying an overhand knot. Repeat twice and trim tail thread.

52 Weave thread to Location 1 on **Fig. 17**. Three tassels of differing lengths will be added in each location.

53 String one 11°, ten 13°, one 11°, ten 13°, one 11°, ten 13°, one 11°, two 13°, a dagger, and two 13° beads.

54 Pass back through the 11° bead. String ten 13° beads and weave back into the next 11° bead. Repeat twice more and weave into the opposite side of the triangle bead of Location 1 on **Fig. 17** (Refer to **Fig. 18** for a side view.)

55 Repeat Steps 53 and 54 for two loop sequences.

56 Repeat Steps 53 and 54 for one loop sequence.

Figure 18

57 Weave to subsequent Locations (2 to 7) as shown in **Fig. 17** and add clusters of fringes as in Steps 53 to 56.

58 Weave thread to Location 8 from the back of the fringework. String one 11°, ten 13°, one 11°, ten 13°, one 11°, ten 13°, one 11°, ten 13°, one 11°, the oval bead, one 11° and three 13° beads (**Figs. 17 and 19**).

Figure 19

59 Weave back into the 11° bead, the oval and the 11° bead. String ten 13° beads and weave into the next 11° bead. Repeat three more times and weave into the opposite side of the triangle bead.

60 Weave down this fringe and pass under the thread of a previous pass. Tie an overhand knot. Repeat twice and trim thread.

61 Repeat Steps 43 to 60 to add fringe to the other side of lariat.

Quatrefoil Renaissance
BRACELET

This bracelet uses a quatrefoil-shaped element along with a triangle medallion element for a dazzling Renaissance-inspired bracelet. A quatrefoil is generally a symmetrical shape of four overlapping circles and was frequently featured in Gothic Revival architecture. The shape is reminiscent of a four-leaf clover, a symbol of good luck. The bracelet is terminated with antique brass bar findings and a coin pearl clasp. The coin pearl is encased in a filigree wrap and converted into a button by weaving seed beads into the base which are connected via jump rings to the bar finding.

MATERIALS

5 g brown iris 15° Japanese seed beads

1 g chartreuse AB 11° Japanese seed beads

1 off-white 12mm freshwater coin pearl

6 off-white 4.5mm freshwater pearls

13 erinite Swarovski 3mm crystal beads

30 chartreuse speckled 3x4mm Czech firepolished rondelles (MC)

5 aqua green luster 3x4mm Czech firepolished rondelles (AC)

1 antique 20x20mm square brass filigree

2 antique 30x12mm acorn leaves brass bar connectors

8 antique 4.75mm brass jump rings

6 lb FireLine

Size 12 beading needles

TOOLS

Chain-nose pliers

Optional: Old wooden ruler or dowel

Flush cutters

Beading mat

SIZE

7.5" (19 cm)

TECHNIQUES

Right-angle weave, flat peyote, reverse picot

CREATING THE QUATREFOIL ELEMENTS

→**1** Start with 24" (61 cm) of FireLine. Pick up a pearl and eight 15° beads. Pass through the opposite end of the pearl **(Fig. 1)**.

→**2** Pick up another eight 15° beads and pass through the opposite end of the pearl **(Fig. 2)**.

→**3** Pass CCW through the first bead on one side.

→**4** Pick up three 15° beads and pass CW into the opposite end of this first bead, creating a reverse RAW picot **(Fig. 3)**. Weave four beads away CCW.

→**5** Repeat Step 4 three more times **(Fig. 4)**.

→**6** Pass through the second bead of the first picot. Pick up seven 15° beads and pass CCW through the second bead of the second picot.

→**7** Repeat Step 6 three times until an outer ring is created around the pearl center **(Fig. 5)**.

→**8** Pass through the first bead of the first set of seven beads added in Step 6. Weave a bead into every other bead for a peyote row. There should be three high beads. Pass though the last bead, the high bead on the second picot, and the first bead on the second seven-bead sequence **(Fig. 6)**.

→**9** Repeat Step 8 three times.

→**10** Pass through the first high bead added in Step 8.

→**11** Pick up five 15° beads and pass through the last high bead of this link sequence.

→**12** Pick up one 15°, one 11°, and one 15° bead into the first high bead of the second sequence **(Fig. 7)**.

→**13** Repeat Steps 11 and 12 three times **(Fig. 8)**.

TIPS

→ Each quatrefoil element and its respective connection rondelles are about 1" (2.5 cm) and the bracelet can be reduced or elongated based on this measurement.

→ Several colors of 15° beads could be used as embellishments to add visual interest.

Figure 1

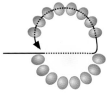

Figure 2

Figure 3

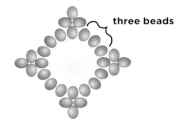

three beads

Figure 4

Figure 5

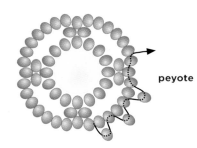

peyote

Figure 6

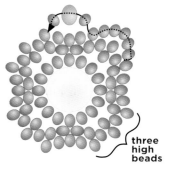

three high beads

Figure 7

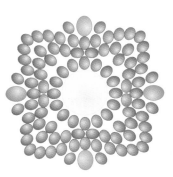

Figure 8

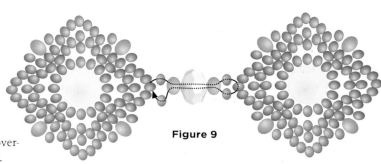

Figure 9

14 Pass under the thread from a previous pass and tie an overhand knot. Leave working thread for connections later.

15 With tail thread, weave through two beads on the inner circle around the pearl. Pass under the thread from a previous pass and tie an overhand knot. Repeat twice and trim thread.

16 Repeat Steps 1 to 15 five more times to make a total of six quartrefoils.

JOINING QUATREFOILS AND CONNECTING TO BAR FINDING

17 With the first quatrefoil, weave thread to the center bead of one corner. This should be the outer five bead edge and the third bead in the sequence. Pick up one 15°, one 11°, one AC rondelle, one 11°, and one 15° bead. Pass through the center bead of the corner of the second quatrefoil **(Fig. 9)**.

18 Pick up one 15° bead and pass back through the 11°, rondelle, and opposing 11° bead. Pick up another 15° bead and pass through the opposite end of the center bead from the first quatrefoil **(Fig. 9)**.

19 Reinforce, this connection by going through all beads once more.

20 Pass under the thread from a previous pass and tie an overhand knot.

21 Weave thread to the first bead of the opposite corner of this connection on the first quatrefoil to connect to the bar finding.

22 Pick up three 15° beads, pass through the center of bar, and pick up another three 15° beads. Pass through the opposite end of the first bead on the quatrefoil. Weave back through the beads just added to reinforce and then back through the first bead toward the direction of the fifth bead in this sequence **(Fig. 10)**.

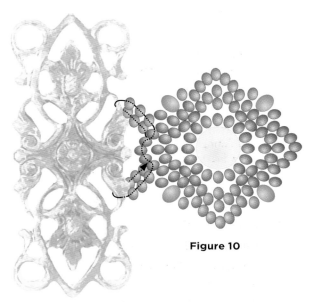

Figure 10

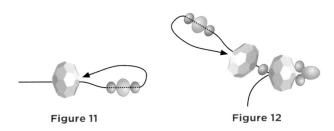

Figure 11

Figure 12

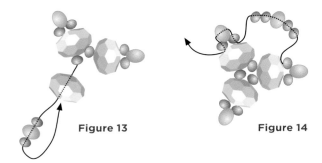

Figure 13

Figure 14

→**23** Repeat Step 22 on the fifth bead to secure this connection.

→**24** Pass through two beads CW, pass under the thread of a previous pass, and tie an overhand knot. Repeat twice and trim thread.

→**25** Repeat Steps 17 to 20 and Step 24 three times to connect three more quatrefoils.

→**26** Repeat Steps 17 to 24 to connect the sixth quatrefoil to the other bar finding.

TRIANGLE RONDELLE MEDALLIONS AND CONNECTING TO QUATREFOIL ELEMENTS

→**27** Start with 24" (61 cm) of FireLine. Pick up a MC rondelle, 15°, 11°, and 15° beads. Pass back through the rondelle creating a picot and leaving a 5" (13 cm) tail **(Fig. 11)**.

→**28** Pick up a 15°, MC rondelle, 15°, 11°, and 15° bead. Pass back through the second rondelle, creating another picot **(Fig. 12)**.

→**29** Repeat Step 28.

→**30** Pick up a 15° bead and pass back through the opposite end of the first rondelle, so the picots are on the outer edge of each of the rondelles. Weave through all beads added in Step 28 **(Fig.13)**.

→**31** Pick up two 15°, one 11°, and two 15° beads and pass through all picot beads on the second rondelle **(Fig. 14)**.

→**32** Repeat Step 31 twice. Weave to the 11° bead of the first picot.

→**33** Pick up three 15° beads and pass through the opposite end of the 11° bead to create a reverse RAW picot **(Fig. 15a)**.

→**34** Weave to the next 11° bead and repeat Step 33 five times **(Fig 15b)**.

→**35** Weave up to the center bead of the first picot created in Step 33.

→**36** Pick up a 15° bead, pass through the 11° bead of the second quatrefoil, and pick up another 15° bead. Pass back through the opposite end of the picot bead from Step 35. Reinforce this connection once more **(Fig. 16)**.

→**37** Weave CCW to the top bead, two picots away from this connection. Repeat Steps 35 and 36 to connect to the first quatrefoil.

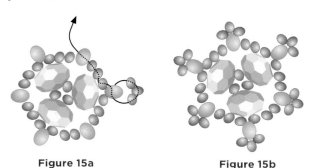

Figure 15a

Figure 15b

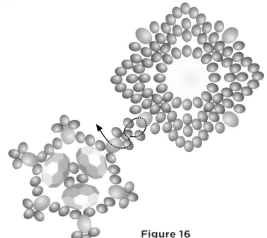

Figure 16

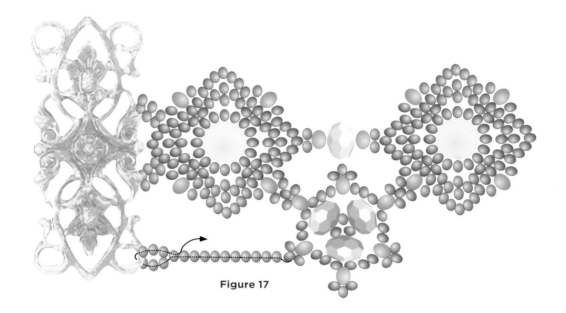

Figure 17

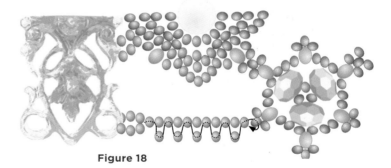

Figure 18

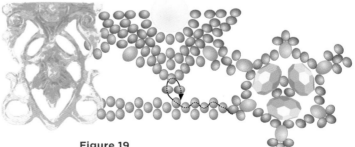

Figure 19

→**38** Weave CCW to the top bead of the next picot. Pick up seventeen 15° beads, weave through the edge loop on the bar finding, and pass back through the eleventh bead just strung **(Fig. 17)**.

→**39** Weave a bead into every other bead to create a peyote row. Weave through the last bead and into the opposite end of the picot from Step 38. There should be three rows beaded and five high beads **(Fig. 18)**.

→**40** Weave through the peyote stitches without adding any beads to the inner third high bead. Pick up one 15° bead and pass through the adjoining center bead of the first quatrefoil **(Fig. 19)**.

→**41** Pick up another 15° bead and pass through the opposite end of the third high bead from the peyote row **(Fig. 19)**.

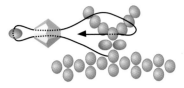

Figure 20a

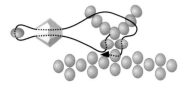

Figure 20b

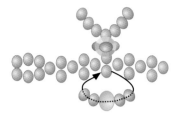

Figure 21

→**42** Pick up a crystal and 15° bead. Pass back through the crystal and to the center edge bead on attached quatrefoil in the opposite orientation **(Fig. 20a)**. To center the crystal, weave CCW into the adjoining RAW link. Weave back through the crystal and 15° bead, then weave back down and into the opposite 15° bead **(Fig. 20b)**.

→**43** Weave through the third bead on the peyote row and weave through all beads connected to the bar finding to reinforce.

→**44** Weave back through the peyote stitches without adding any beads to the outer third high bead. String two 15°, one 11° and two 15° beads. Weave back through the opposite end of the third bead on the peyote row for a reverse RAW picot **(Fig. 21)**.

→**45** Pass under the thread from a previous pass and tie a knot. Repeat twice and trim thread.

→**46** Repeat Steps 27 to 45 three times to connect the other three edge medallions.

→**47** Repeat Steps 27 to 45 for the remaining six medallions, keeping in mind that the inner medallion connections have peyote starts that are only eleven beads, not seventeen. Six extra beads were required to create the looped links to the bar finding, which are not required for the internal connections.

CREATING THE BUTTON CLOSURE

→**48** With the square filigree, hold coin pearl with index finger and thumb at center. Start the wrap on each of the four corners by bending slightly with pressure on your beading pad. Once started, use your chain-nose pliers to complete the wrap and carefully secure the coin pearl. Use a wooden surface to burnish, as necessary.

→**49** With 12" (30.5 cm) of FireLine, weave through the center of the filigree from the back. Pick up five 15° beads and weave into the filigree from the opposite side.

→**50** Pass through the beads just strung again. Pass under the thread from a previous pass and tie an overhand knot.

→**51** Repeat Step 50 twice more and trim thread.

→**52** With tail thread, Repeat Step 50 twice and trim thread.

→**53** Attach two jump rings to the center of the bar clasp. Join these two rings with another jump ring, ensuring that this ring is connected from the back of bar clasp.

→**54** Add another jump ring to link created in Step 53.

→**55** Add another jump ring to link created in Step 54.

→**56** Connect link made in Step 55 to the loop on back of the coin pearl **(Fig. 22)**.

CREATING THE LOOP CLOSURE

→ **57** With 24" (61 cm) of FireLine, string one 11° and five 15° beads. Pass back through the 11° bead, leaving a 5" (13 cm) tail; tie a square knot.

→ **58** Pick up thirty-five 15° beads **(Fig. 23)**. Pass through all beads from Step 57, back up the 11°, and into the first 15° bead of the thirty-five-bead sequence.

→ **59** Pick up a 15° bead and pass through the third bead. Repeat for eight high beads **(Fig. 24)**.

→ **60** Pick up a crystal and 15° bead. Pass back through the crystal. Skip a bead and bead into the next bead **(Fig. 25)**.

→ **61** Repeat Step 59 eight times to mirror the peyote stitches on complementary side.

→ **62** Pass through last bead into the 11° and reinforce the connection loop back up through the 11° bead. Pass under thread from a previous pass and tie an overhand knot. Weave through two beads, repeat twice and trim thread.

→ **63** With tail thread, pass under thread from a previous pass and tie an overhand knot. Pass through two beads, repeat twice and trim thread.

→ **64** Attach two jump rings to the center of the bar clasp. Join these two rings with another jump ring, ensuring that this ring is connected from the back of the bar clasp.

→ **65** Connect link made in Step 64 to the smaller beaded loop.

Figure 23

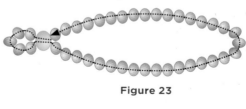

Figure 24

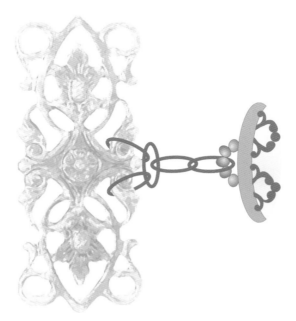

Figure 22

Figure 25

Victorian Diamond
CUFF

This design first originated with the single diamond component. Initially, the bracelet was to have an airy appearance with the diamonds connected only by their corners. However, it was too fragile for a cuff bracelet. With some experimentation, ruffled pearl components were created in the center of four diamonds to add structure. This bracelet shows the versatility of using RAW and reverse picots, two stitches I often use together for connecting two or more elements and for embellishments in lacy designs. The margaritas liven up the bracelet, and the snap closures create a seamless cuff.

MATERIALS
8 g brown iris 15° Japanese seed beads (MC)

1 g bronze metallic 15° Japanese seed beads for the top of margaritas (AC)

5 g brown iris Japanese 11° seed beads (MC)

2 g matte cranberry bronze Japanese 11° seed beads (AC)

30 tabac 6mm Swarovski 3700 margarita beads

120 copper bronze 3x4mm freshwater rondelle pearls

20 copper bronze 5mm freshwater pearls

2 black size 3 sew-on snaps

6 lb FireLine

Size 12 beading needles

TOOL
Ruler (optional)

Flush cutters

SIZE
7" (18 cm)

TECHNIQUES
Right-angle weave, reverse picot

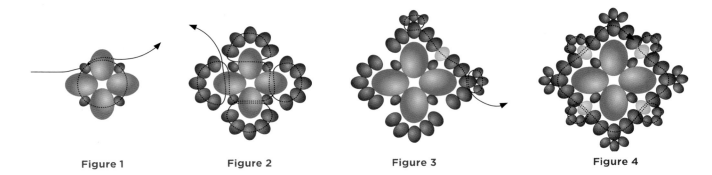

| Figure 1 | Figure 2 | Figure 3 | Figure 4 |

THE FIRST DIAMOND MEDALLION

→**1** Start with 24" (61 cm) of FireLine. Pick up one 15° MC bead and one rondelle pearl four times. Tie into a circle with an overhand knot, leaving a 6" (15.5 cm) tail thread. Pass through the adjacent pearl **(Fig. 1)**.

→**2** Pick up five 11° MC beads and pass through the pearl just exited again so that the five beads circle around the first pearl. Pass through the 15° bead and into the next pearl.

→**3** Repeat Step 2 three times **(Fig. 2)**.

→**4** On the last five bead loop, weave to the third bead (center) bead of the beads just added; flip beadwork.

→**5** Pick up three 15° MC beads and pass through the opposite end of the third bead from Step 4. Pass through the fourth and fifth beads into the first gap between two pearls.

→**6** Pick up one 11° AC bead and pass through the first bead of the next five-bead loop into the third (or center) bead **(Fig. 3)**.

→**7** Repeat Steps 5 and 6 three times. Weave back to the first 11° AC bead added in Step 6.

→**8** Pick up three 15° MC beads and pass through the opposite end of the 11° AC bead from Step 7. Weave to the next 11° AC bead.

→**9** Repeat Step 8 three times **(Fig. 4)**.

→**10** Pass under the thread from a previous pass and tie an overhand knot. Weave through two beads, repeat twice and trim thread.

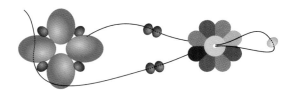

Figure 5

TIPS

→ Although the project is for a five-row cuff, a smaller version can be made with a three-row cuff and one snap closure.

→ The size of the rondelle pearls will determine the amount of components necessary. You can shorten the bracelet length by using smaller freshwater rondelles. Use your ruler to check the length.

→ For a less glitzy bracelet, margaritas can be omitted from the center of each diamond. Also, any flat embellishment no larger than 6mm can be substituted for an alternate look.

11 With tail thread, pick up two 15° MC beads, the margarita, and a 15° AC bead. Weave back through the margarita and pick up two more 15° MC beads. Weave into the opposite pearl in reverse orientation **(Fig. 5)**.

12 Pass through a 15° MC bead and pick up two 15° MC beads. Pass back through the margarita and the 15° AC bead. Weave back through the margarita and pick up another two 15° MC beads. Weave into the opposite pearl in reverse orientation **(Fig. 6)**.

13 Weave through the first two beads of the complementary pearl's five-bead loop. Pass under the thread from a previous pass and tie an overhand knot. Pass through two beads, repeat twice and trim thread.

THE SECOND AND THIRD DIAMOND MEDALLION

The second and subsequent diamond medallions will share two or more reverse picot accents with its adjacent neighbor(s). The corner picots are also connection points that will form the space needed to later add the ruffled pearl accents, giving the bracelet balance and structure.

14 Repeat Steps 1 to 4 on the first medallion.

15 Pick up one 15° MC bead and weave CW into the top picot bead of one of the corners of the first medallion. Pick up another 15° MC bead and pass through the opposite end of the 11° MC bead from the second medallion **(Fig. 7)**.

16 Since this is a connection point, pass through all beads once more to reinforce. Pass through the fourth and fifth 11° beads into the first gap between two pearls.

17 Repeat Steps 6 and 5 three times.

18 Repeat Step 6.

19 Weave back to the first 11° AC bead added in Step 17. Repeat Steps 8 to 13.

20 Repeat Steps 14 to 19 for the third diamond medallion, connecting the common picot opposite the first and second diamond connections. This creates a three-diamond medallion strip.

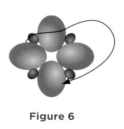

Figure 6

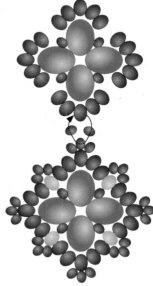

Figure 7

FOURTH DIAMOND MEDALLION

→**21** Repeat Steps 1 to 4.

→**22** Pick up one 15° MC bead and weave CW into the top picot bead (at 3 o'clock) of the third medallion. Pick up another 15° MC bead and pass through the opposite end of the 11° MC bead from the fourth medallion **(Fig. 8)**.

→**23** Repeat Step 16.

→**24** Repeat Steps 6 and 5 three times.

→**25** Repeat Step 6.

→**26** Weave back to the first 11° AC bead added in Step 24. Repeat Steps 8 to 13.

FIFTH DIAMOND MEDALLION AND RUFFLED PEARL CENTER

→**27** Repeat Steps 1 to 4.

→**28** Pick up one 15° MC bead and weave CW into the top picot bead (at 6 o'clock) of the fourth medallion. Pick up another 15° MC bead and pass through the opposite end of the 11° MC bead from the fifth medallion **(Fig. 8)**.

→**29** Repeat Step 16.

→**30** Repeat Step 6.

→**31** Pick up one 15° MC bead and weave CW into the top picot bead (at 3 o'clock) of the second medallion. Pick up another 15° MC bead and pass through the opposite end of the 11° MC bead from the fifth medallion.

→**32** Repeat Step 16.

→**33** Repeat Steps 6 and 5 twice.

→**34** Repeat Step 6.

→**35** Weave back to the first 11° AC bead added in Step 30. Repeat Steps 8 and 9.

→**36** Pass through the second (center) bead of the first picot added in Step 35. Pick up one 11° MC, one 11° AC, and one 11° MC bead. Weave into the top picot of the fourth medallion **(Fig. 9)**.

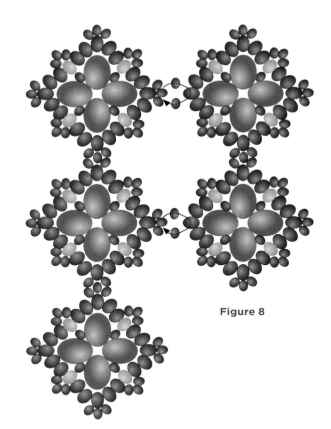

Figure 8

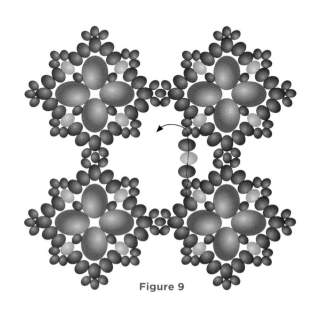

Figure 9

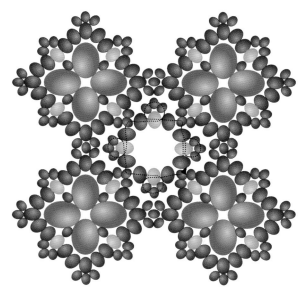

Figure 10

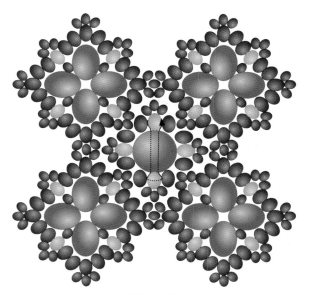

Figure 11a

Figure 11b

→**37** Repeat Step 36 three more times, connecting the top picot bead to adjoining diamond medallions to form a circle.

→**38** Weave to the 11° AC bead added in Step 36. Pick up three 15° MC beads and pass through the opposite end of the 11° AC bead for a reverse RAW picot.

→**39** Repeat Step 38 three times to add reverse RAW picots to the remaining 11° AC beads **(Fig. 10)**.

→**40** Weave CCW to the second 11° AC bead (at 12 o'clock). Pick up a freshwater pearl and pass through the opposite 11° AC bead (at 6 o'clock). Pass back through the pearl and into the opposite end of the 11° AC bead **(Figs. 11a and 11b)**. Pass back through the pearl and the 11° AC bead.

→**41** Pick up three 15° beads and pass through the opposite end of the 11° AC bead again. Pass through CCW to the top bead of the next picot.

→**42** Pick up three 15° beads and pass through the opposite end of the top bead of the picot. Pass through the next 11° AC bead. **(Fig. 12)**.

→**43** Repeat Steps 41 and 42 three more times.

→**44** Repeat Steps 10 to 13.

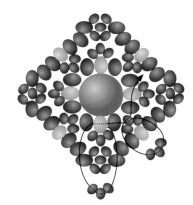

Figure 12

ALL OTHER SUBSEQUENT DIAMOND MEDALLIONS

Repeat adding medallions and ruffled pearls to the respective adjoining components by attaching through common picots by following the guidelines of the previous section until only two freshwater pearls are left. There should be ten columns of diamond medallions. The pearl ruffles are added at the center of four diamond medallions.

SNAPS

I wanted to design a seamless cuff so the design has a nice flow. The bottom snap is sewn facing up and the top snap is sewn facing down with a pearl embellishment on top. The two will overlap for a seamless hidden clasp.

BOTTOM SNAP

→**45** Weave CCW into the second (center) bead of the inner picot.

→**46** Pick up one 11° MC, one 11° AC, and one 11° MC bead. Weave into the top picot of inner picot of the adjoining medallion.

→**47** Pick up one 11° MC, one 11° AC, one 11° MC, one 15° MC, one 11° MC, one 11° AC, one 11° MC, one 15° MC, one 11° MC, one 11° AC, and one 11° MC bead. Weave into the top picot bead from Step 45 to form a circle **(Fig. 13)**.

→**48** Pass through to the first 11° AC bead and string three 15° MC beads. Weave into the opposite end of 11° AC bead.

→**49** Pass through to the second 11° AC bead and string one 15° MC bead. Weave into the first bead of the picot right above. String another 15° MC bead and weave into the opposite end of the 11° AC bead. As this is a connection point, weave through all beads once more to reinforce **(Fig. 14)**.

→**50** Repeat Step 48 for the next 11° AC bead and Step 49 for remaining 11° AC bead.

→**51** The snap is sewn and attached from the top picots and at the 15° MC beads of the ring. Face one half of the snap so it is sewn facing up.

→**52** Pass through the top bead of the first adjoining picot and into one of the four crevices on the snap. Weave into the opposite end of the same picot bead (**Fig. 15** for locations of securing the snap).

→**53** Re-enforce Step 52 twice more **(Fig. 16)**.

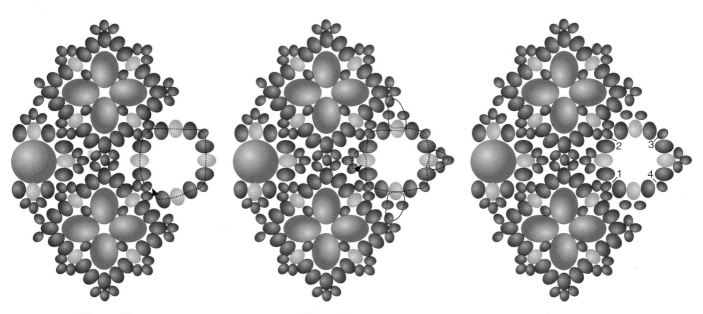

Figure 13   **Figure 14**   **Figure 15**

54 Pick up three 15° MC beads and weave into the opposite end of the same picot bead **(Fig. 17)**.

55 Repeat Step 48 on first 11° AC bead.

56 Repeat Steps 52 to 55 three more times to attach the remaining three crevices of the snap to the base ring on Locations 2, 3, and 4 **(Fig. 17)**. The 15° MC bead at Locations 3 and 4 act as the top bead of a picot.

57 Weave into the closest medallion. Latch onto the thread from a previous pass and tie an overhand knot. Pass through two beads, repeat twice and trim thread.

58 Repeat Steps 45 to 57 for other bottom snap.

TOP SNAP

59 Repeat Steps 45 to 50.

60 The snap is sewn and attached from the top picots and the 15° MC beads of the ring. Face the complementary half of the snap so it is sewn facing down.

61 Repeat Steps 52 to 56.

62 Weave to the first 11° AC bead. Pick up a freshwater pearl and pass through the opposite 11° AC bead. Pass back through the pearl and into the opposite end of the 11° AC bead **(Fig. 18-a and 18-b)**.

63 Repeat Step 57.

64 Repeat Steps 59 to 63 for other top snap.

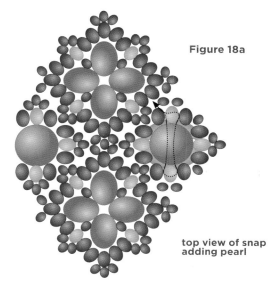

Figure 18a

top view of snap adding pearl

Figure 18b

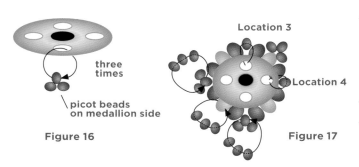

three times

picot beads on medallion side

Figure 16

Location 3

Location 4

Figure 17

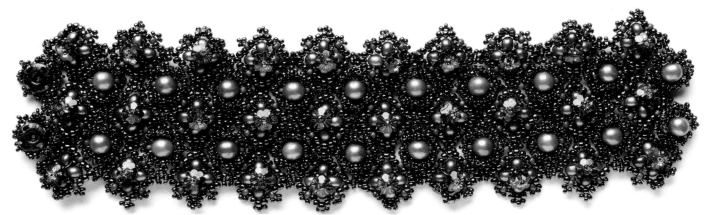

Triple Spiral Garden
LARIAT

Lariats are so feminine, and I love wearing them as well as making them. This particular design came about as I was creating texture with a triple spiral stitch. I kept on beading and beading. Before long I had a length of rope perfect to incorporate as a lariat. The Russian-style beaded leaves are created with 11° and 15° beads.

MATERIALS
LARIAT

45 g each of chartreuse-lined aqua, transparent chartreuse luster, and dark sage luster 15° Japanese seed beads

30 g 11° Japanese seed beads (in same colors as 15°)

15 g teal-lined topaz 11° Toho Japanese triangle beads

40 g transparent chartreuse luster 8° Japanese seed beads

500 olivine luster 3mm Czech firepolished beads

500 lt. olivine 3mm Swarovski bicone beads

LEAVES

5 g each of chartreuse-lined aqua, transparent chartreuse luster, and dark sage 15° Japanese seed beads

2 g 11° Japanese seed beads (in same colors as 15°)

FLOWERS

5 g each of fuchsia-lined crystal, cranberry AB, and berry topaz AB silver-lined 15° Japanese seed beads

4 g chartreuse-lined aqua 15° Japanese seed beads for the flower center

BERRY CLUSTERS

12 each of lavender, cranberry, and rose 5mm freshwater pearls

6 each of lavender, cranberry, and rose 6mm freshwater pearls

6 lb FireLine

Silamide thread

Size 12 beading needle

TOOLS
Chain-nose pliers, flush cutters, No-tangle thread bobbin, beeswax, ruler

SIZE
57" (145 cm)

TECHNIQUES
Decreasing peyote, right-angle weave, triple spiral, branch fringe

TRIPLE SPIRAL ROPE

The triple spiral is made in the same way as a single or double spiral. Using size 8° seed beads as the core allows for multiple passes. Each colorway set is woven through the same core beads at each iteration. The following abbreviations will be used for each C (colorway).

→**1** Start with 3 yd (274.5 cm) of FireLine. From the center, wrap half of the FireLine onto the bobbin. This method will reduce the necessity to add thread too often since the spiral stitch can be woven from both ends.

→**2** Start with C1. String four 8° beads, three 15°, one 11°, one triangle, one 11°, and three 15°. Tie into a circle with an overhand knot. Pass up through all four core beads **(Fig. 1)**.

→**3** Switch to C2. Pick up three 15°, one 11°, one firepolished, one 11°, and three 15° beads. Pass through the same four 8° beads from Step 2 **(Fig. 2)**.

→**4** Switch to C3 and repeat Step 3 **(Fig. 3)**.

→**5** In every sequence the thread will pass through four core beads. As you bead the beadwork will spiral up so the beads just added will be to your left. To keep the three colorways spiraling uniformly, the previous row of each colorway will always be to the left of your current beading in that

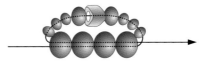

Figure 1

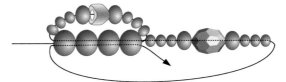

Figure 2

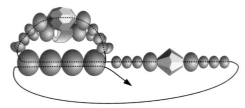

Figure 3

C1:

15° seed, 11° seed, and 11° triangle.

C2:

15° seed, 11° seed, and 3mm Czech firepolished bead.

C3:

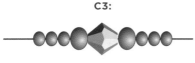

15° seed, 11° seed, and 3mm Swarovski bicone crystal.

TIPS

→ Although pearls are used for the berry clusters, you can easily incorporate any beads in a complementary color palette.

→ 1" (2.5 cm) of beading will incorporate about ten each of the triangle, firepolished, and crystal beads. Keep this in mind when purchasing your materials if you'd like to reduce the length of the lariat.

colorway. Only C1 will have an additional 8° bead added in the stringing sequence with C2 and C3 woven through the same core beads.

→**6** Switch to C1. String one 8° bead and C1 beads. Pass through the top three core beads and the 8° bead just strung.

→**7** Repeat Steps 3 and 4.

→**8** Repeat Steps 6 to 7 to build length to the spiral. Unwind thread from bobbin to continue beading for a total of 50", adding thread as necessary through the outside spiral beads. Weave all threads off through the outside spiral beads by passing under the thread from a previous pass and tie an overhand knot. Repeat twice and trim thread.

MAKING THE LEAVES

Using 11° and 15° beads on the first two peyote rows, with proper thread tension, creates a slight curvature to the beadwork. By implementing three rows of peyote decreases, an attractive leaf shape emerges. Connecting two matched pairs and adding leaf veins completes the leaf.

→**9** Using 24" (61 cm) of FireLine, string twenty-six beads alternating between 15° and 11° beads in C1. Start with 15° and end with an 11° bead. Use a stop bead if necessary, leaving a 6" tail.

→**10** Pick up a 15° bead and pass through the last 15° bead just strung to begin the third row of peyote stitch. Continue adding a 15° bead and passing through every other bead. There should be thirteen beads added. Pull thread so that the beadwork will curve slightly **(Fig. 4)**.

→**11** Pick up a 15° bead and weave into the high beads added in Step 10 for twelve iterations **(Fig. 5)**.

→**12** Pass through the twenty-fourth bead on the first row and then last bead added in Step 11 to turn beadwork. Pull tight so the thread will snap in between beadwork without showing **(Fig. 6)**.

Figure 4

Figure 5

twenty-fourth bead

Figure 6

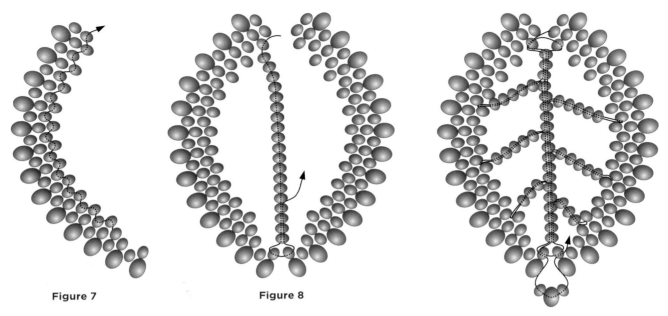

Figure 7   Figure 8

Figure 9

→**13** Pick up a 15° bead and pass through the high beads added in Step 11 for eleven iterations. This completes the fifth peyote row **(Fig. 7)**.

→**14** Pass through the edge beads. Pass under the thread from a previous pass and tie an overhand knot. Repeat twice and trim thread. Repeat for the tail thread and set aside.

→**15** Repeat Steps 9 to 14 for a second leaf side but do not tie off working thread.

→**16** Weave into the complementary last bead of the fifth row on the first leaf side. Pick up nineteen 15° beads and pass through the first 15° bead of the third row. Weave up to the complementary 15° bead on the opposite side and up through four of the nineteen beads just strung **(Fig. 8)**.

→**17** The veins will range from three to five 15° beads depending on your thread tension when creating the initial curvature of the leaf in Step 10. This is visually determined by how steep you want the leaf veins to appear in the final leaf. Generally there are three to four beads on the bottom veins and four to five beads on the widest part of the leaf **(Fig. 9)**.

→**18** Pick up three 15° beads and angle towards one of the leaf sides. Pass under the thread from the last row of beading and pass back through the beads just added.

→**19** Pass back through five core beads and add a second vein.

→**20** Repeat Steps 18 and 19 to add a third vein increasing from three to five beads, as necessary. Three veins on either side of the leaf core will make for a pleasing leaf. Weave up five beads and through the last 15° bead to secure the core vein. Pass through the complementary 15° bead on the opposite side.

→**21** Pass back through three core beads and add a vein. Pass back through the beads just added.

→**22** Pass through five core beads and add another vein. Pass back through the beads just added.

→**23** Pass through four core beads and add the last vein. Pass back through the beads just added.

→**24** Weave down to the 15° beads from the third row of beading to secure the core vein. Pick up one 15°, one 11°, and one 15° bead. Pass back through the complementary 15° bead on the opposite side **(Fig. 9)**.

→**25** Weave thread through the outer edge of leaf. Pass under the thread from a previous pass and tie an overhand knot. Repeat twice and trim thread.

→**26** Repeat Steps 9 to 25 to make five additional leaves in C1, six leaves in C2, and six leaves in C3.

Figure 10

Figure 11

Figure 12

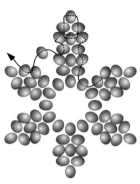

Figure 13

MAKING THE FLOWERS

→**27** Using 24" (61 cm) of Silamide, pick up twelve flower center 15° beads and tie into a circle with a square knot. Pass through two beads away from the knot **(Fig. 10)**.

→**28** Pick up three 15° beads and pass through the opposite side of the 15° for a reverse picot. Pass through the next two beads, CCW. Repeat five times **(Fig. 11)**.

→**29** Pass through the first 15° seed bead of the picot, pick up one flower color 15°, and pass through the top picot bead. Continuing with the flower color 15°, pick up three beads and pass through the opposite end of the top picot bead. Pick up one 15° bead and pass back through the third 15° bead of the first row's picot. Pass through the first bead of the next picot **(Fig. 12)**. Repeat around.

→**30** Weave thread up through the first bead of the second picot row. Repeat Step 29 to add a picot on top of the picot in the previous round. Pick up a 15° seed bead and pass through the first bead of the next picot on the previous round. Repeat around **(Fig. 13)**.

→**31** Weave down into the center of beadwork into the original twelve beads from Step 27. Weave into a bead between the picots created in Step 28 to make this layer of petals alternate with the first layer.

→**32** Repeat Steps 28 to 29 for a smaller inner flower level. Weave down into the center of beadwork. Pass under the thread from a previous pass and tie an overhand knot. Repeat twice and trim thread.

→**33** Make six flowers in each of the three colorways.

ADDING THE FRINGE

→**34** Start with 1.5 yd (137.5 cm) of FireLine and add thread to the rope through the outer spiral beads. Pass through several spiral beads and tie a half hitch knot. Weave through several beads, repeat with another knot. Repeat once more and trim tail thread. Weave thread to exit out of the 11° bead of the last set of spiral stitches.

→**35** Select only one color from the three colorways for use throughout the fringework. Pick up three 11° beads and weave into the complementary next 11° bead of the spiral. Repeat twice more to create a ring for the fringe to be attached to.

→**36** Weave thread into the second bead of each of the three beads added to start the fringe. String forty 11° beads for the fringe core **(Fig. 14)**.

→**37** To add leaves, pick up one 11° and two 15° beads and pass through the first 15° bead on the leaf from the second peyote row, with thread path facing toward the center. Pick up one 11° bead (same color as the leaf color) and pass through the complementary 15° bead on the opposite side. Pick up two 15° beads and pass back through the 11° and five core beads. Branch out to add the next component.

→**38** To add pearl clusters, string one 11°, six 15°, a 6mm pearl, and three 15° beads. Pass back through the pearl and two 15° beads. Branch out by picking up two 15° beads, a 5mm pearl, and three 15° beads. Pass back through the pearl and four 15° beads. Branch out and repeat adding the second 5mm pearl to complete the cluster. Pass back through five core beads. Branch out to add the next component.

→**39** To add the flowers, pick up one 11° bead, two 15° beads, the 15° bead in between the larger petals, and two 15° beads. Pass back through the 11° bead and five core beads.

→**40** Alternate between the three colored leaves, flowers, and berry clusters. At the end of the first fringe, pass through the opposite end of the second bead in Step 36. Weave to the second bead on the next set of the three beads added in Step 35.

→**41** Repeat Steps 36 to 40 for a second and third fringe. Changing the order of the components on each fringe creates a tiered effect and adds visual interest.

→**42** Weave the thread into the spiral beads. Pass under a thread from a previous pass and tie an overhand knot. Weave through several beads and repeat with another knot. Repeat once more and trim thread.

→**43** Repeat Steps 34 to 42 to add fringe to the other side of lariat.

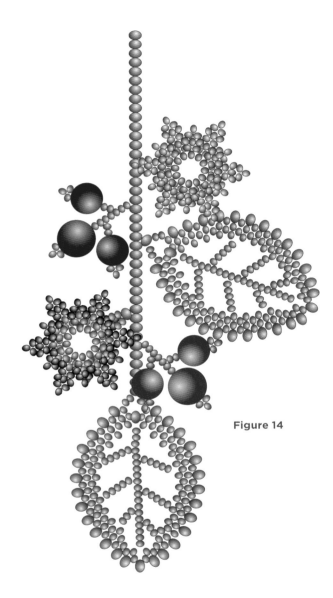

Figure 14

TECHNIQUES

OVERHAND KNOT

Make a loop and pass the cord that lies behind the loop over the front cord and through the loop. Pull tight.

SQUARE KNOT

The square knot is the classic sturdy knot for securing most stringing materials. First make an overhand knot, passing the right end over the left end. Next, make another overhand knot, this time passing the left end over the right end. Pull tight.

HALF HITCH KNOT

Half hitch knots may be worked with two or more strands—one strand is knotted over one or more other strands. Form a loop around the cord(s). Pull the end through the loop just formed and pull tight. Repeat for the length of cord you want to cover.

Half Hitch Knot Between Beads

OPENING AND CLOSING JUMP RINGS

To open a jump ring, grasp each side of its opening with a pair of pliers. Don't pull apart. Instead, twist in opposite directions to avoid distorting the shape. To close, twist the sides of the jump ring back together with the pliers.

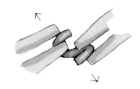

WRAPPED LOOP

Begin with a 90° bend at least 2" (5 cm) from the end of the wire. Use round-nose pliers to form a loop with a tail overlapping the bend. Wrap the tail tightly down the neck of the wire to create a couple of coils. Trim the excess wire to finish.

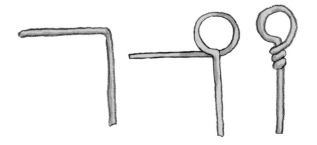

WRAPPED LOOP ON TOP-DRILLED BEADS

Wrapped loop bails turn top-drilled beads, usually teardrops, into pendants. Center the bead on a 3" or longer piece of wire. Bend both ends of the wire up the sides and across the top of the bead. Bend one end straight up at the center of the bead, then wrap the other wire around it to form a few coils. Form a wrapped loop with the straight-up wire, wrapping it back down over the already formed coils. Trim the excess wire.

NETTING (SINGLE NEEDLE)

Begin by stringing a base row of thirteen beads.
String five beads and go back through the fifth bead
from the end of the base row. String another five
beads, skip three beads of the base row, and go back
through the next; repeat to the end of the row. To
turn, pass back through the last three beads (one leg
of the last net). String five beads, pass back through
the center bead of the next net, and continue.

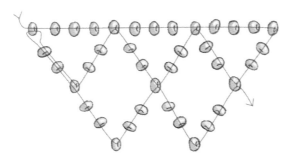

RIGHT-ANGLE WEAVE (SINGLE NEEDLE)

String four beads and pass through the first three
beads again to form the first unit. For the rest of the
row, string three beads, pass through the last bead
passed through in the previous unit, and the first
two just strung; the thread path will resemble a

figure eight, alternating directions with each unit.
To begin the next row, pass through beads to exit the
side of the last unit. String three beads, pass through
the last bead passed through, and the first bead just
strung. *String two beads, pass through the next
edge bead of the previous row, the last bead passed
through in the previous unit, and the last two beads
just strung. Pass through the next edge bead of the
previous row, string two beads, pass through the last
bead of the previous unit, the edge bead just passed
through, and the first bead just strung. Repeat from
* to complete the row, then begin a new row as
before.

SPIRAL ROPE

The basic formula for a spiral rope has larger beads
as the center core with smaller and more beads in
the outer loops. Begin with 4A (core) and 5B (loop)
beads. Pass through the A beads again, forming a D
shape. String 1A and 5B; pass through the top 3A and
the 1A just strung. Repeat, stringing 1A and 5B, and
passing through the top 4A for each stitch.

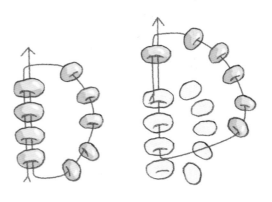

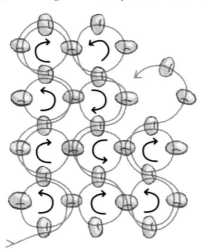

LADDER STITCH

Thread a needle on each end of the thread and pass one needle through one or more beads from left to right and pass the other needle through the same beads from right to left. Continue adding beads by crisscrossing both needles through one bead at a time. Use this stitch to make strings of beads or as the foundation for brick or Ndebele stitch.

To work a single-needle ladder stitch, string two beads and pass through them again. String one bead. Pass through the last stitched bead and the one just strung. Repeat, adding one bead at a time and working in a figure-eight pattern.

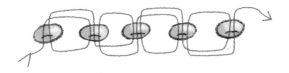

BRICK STITCH

Begin by creating a foundation row in ladder stitch. String one bead and pass through the closest exposed loop of the foundation row. Pass back through the same bead and continue, adding one bead at a time.

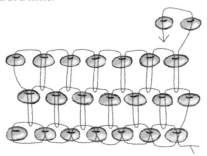

FLAT NDEBELE (HERRINGBONE)

Begin with a foundation row of even-count ladder stitch. String two beads, pass down through the second-to-last bead in the ladder, and up through the next bead. String two beads, pass down the next bead and then up through the following. Repeat to the end of the row. To end the row, pass back through the last bead strung. To begin the next row, string two beads and pass down through the second-to-last bead of the previous row and up through the following bead. Repeat, stringing two beads per stitch and passing down then up through two beads of the previous row. The two-bead stitch will cause the beads to angle-up in each column, like a herringbone fabric.

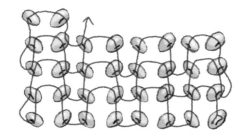

FLAT CIRCULAR NDEBELE (HERRINGBONE)

If there is an odd count, start **(A)**, then add one bead between each **(B)** and then two beads between each of those **(C)**. Increases generally occur in three rows of beading. Weave through one bead, string two beads, and weave down the adjacent bead. String one bead and up the second pair of two beads. Repeat around **(D)**. On next sequence, repeat but instead of stringing one bead, string two in between each Ndebele pair of beads **(E)**. The third row of increases treats the two beads added as an Ndebele pair of beads **(F)**. Next, weave a regular Ndebele row in between each sequence of increases for a smoother transition.

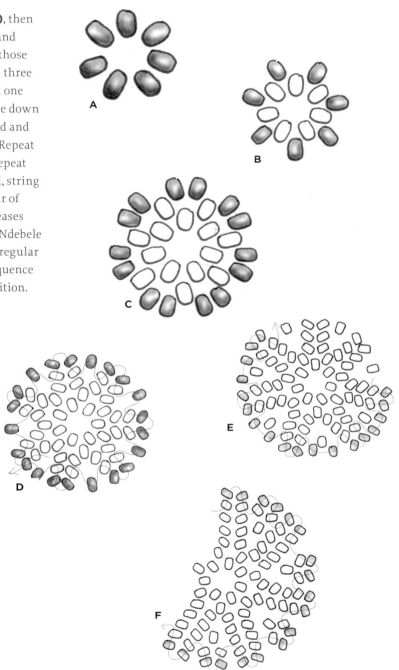

EVEN FLAT PEYOTE

One-drop peyote stitch begins by stringing an even number of beads to create the first two rows. Begin the third row by stringing one bead and passing through the second-to-last bead of the previous rows. String another bead and pass through the fourth-to-last bead of the previous rows. Continue adding one bead at a time, passing over every other bead of the previous rows.

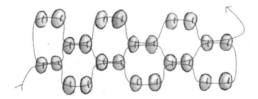

Two-drop peyote stitch is worked the same as above but with two beads at a time instead of one.

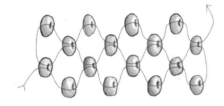

CIRCULAR PEYOTE

String three beads and form the first round by passing through the first bead. For the second round, string two beads and pass through the next bead of the previous round; repeat twice. To step up for the next round, pass through the first bead of the current round. For the third round, string one bead and pass through the next bead of the previous round; repeat all around, then step up at the end of the round. Continue in this manner, alternating the two rounds. You may need to adjust the bead count depending on the relative size of the beads in order to keep the circle flat.

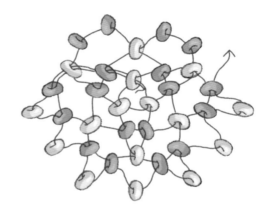

DECREASING PEYOTE

To make a mid-project decrease, simply pass thread through two beads without adding a bead in the "gap." In the next row, work a regular one-drop peyote over the decrease. Keep tension taut to avoid holes.

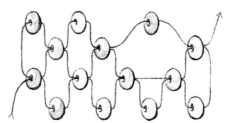

PICOT

To make a picot, string three **(A)** or five **(B)** beads and weave into the next high bead. This sequence is woven into the gaps of edge beading to create a lacey effect and is sometimes used to transition to decreasing stitches.

A

B

REVERSE PICOT

To make a reverse picot, string three **(A)** or five **(B)** beads and weave into the opposite end of the same high bead just exited then down the bead adjoining two adjacent high beads, so thread does not show. Reverse picots are also described as right-angle-weave links.

An alternate version is to hide the gap between two reverse picots by weaving a bead in between **(C)**.

A
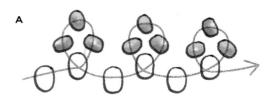

B
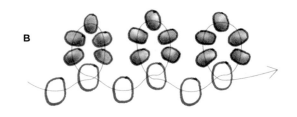

C
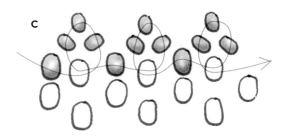

PROJECT RESOURCES

Scalloped Chain Necklace p.14

Aquamarine rondelles: California Collection

Faceted citrine: Amulete Unlimited

Cornerless cubes: Anil Kumar

Ndebele Pearl Medallion Earrings and Linked Bracelet p. 18

Seed beads: Out on a Whim

Seed beads, bead caps, margaritas: San Gabriel Bead Company

Coin freshwater pearls: Evergreen Trading Company

Faceted carnelian beads and drops: A&P Trading/House of Gems

Cornerless cubes: Anil Kumar

Ear wires with inlaid stones: Nina Designs

Netted Rivoli Chain Earrings p. 24

Seed beads, crystals, chain, rivoli rhinestones: San Gabriel Bead Company

Rivoli rhinestones: Beading in the Rain

Seed beads: Out on a Whim

Leverbacks: Rio Grande

Pearl Cascade Necklace p. 30

Crystals: San Gabriel Bead Company

MOP flowers: Pearlbella Trading Company

Pearls: Evergreen Trading Company

Daisy spacers, star bead caps, cornerless cubes: Anil Kumar

Slider clasp: Rio Grande

V Scallop Necklace p. 34

Seed Beads: Out on a Whim

Seed beads, crystals: San Gabriel Bead Company

Toho cubes: Bead Cache

Freshwater pearls: Evergreen Trading Company

Mesh Pearl Bracelet p. 40

Freshwater pearls: Lisa Kan Designs

Italian wire mesh: Specialty Beads

Cornerless cubes: Anil Kumar

Toggles: Rio Grande

Ndebele Twist Band with Floral Center p. 44

Seed beads: Out on a Whim

Seed beads, flower bead, bead cap, Swarovski rondelle: San Gabriel Bead Company

Bohemian Drop Earrings p. 54

Coin pearls: Evergreen Trading Company

Jump rings, filigree, and beadcaps: Vintaj Natural Brass Co.

Seed beads, Czech rondelles, Swarovski crystals: San Gabriel Bead Company

Seed beads: Jane's Fiber and Beads and Out on a Whim

Rivoli Y Drop Necklace p. 60

Seed beads: Out on a Whim

Seed beads, rivolis, crystal drop, firepolished beads: San Gabriel Bead Company

Quatrefoil Nouveau Festoon Necklace p. 68

Nouveau drop bead: Lisa Kan Designs

Coin and freshwater pearls: Evergreen Trading Company

Jump rings, chain, clasp, filigree, wrap findings: Vintaj Natural Brass Co.

Seed beads, Czech rondelles, Swarovski crystals: San Gabriel Bead Company

Seed beads: Jane's Fiber and Beads and Out on a Whim

Double-Sided Maiden Necklace p. 76

Double-sided Cabochon: Kelly Russell-Beadfuddled

Seed pearls: Ancient Moon Beads

Seed beads, flower beads, druk beads: San Gabriel Bead Company

Medici Rhinestone Necklace p. 84

Freshwater pearls: Lisa Kan Designs

Seed beads, glassbeads, Czech firepolished, bead caps, rivoli rhinestones: San Gabriel Bead Company

Seed beads: Out on a Whim

Rivoli rhinestones: Beading in the Rain

Vintage 4671 square octagon rhinestones: Gregory Benson

Deco Collar with Gemstone Drops p. 94

Gemstone drops: Amulete Unlimited and Anil Kumar

Bead cap, clasp: Ezel Jewels

Seed beads, rubber cord, crystals: San Gabriel Bead Company

Seed beads: Jane's Fiber and Beads and Out on a Whim

Charlottes: Garden of Beadin'

Black Lace Lariat p. 100

Charlottes, Czech firepolished, glass beads, daggers: San Gabriel Bead Company

Charlottes: Garden of Beadin'

Quatrefoil Renaissance Bracelet p. 108

Coin and freshwater pearls: Evergreen Trading Company

Jump rings, filigree, bar finding: Vintaj Natural Brass Co.

Seed beads, Czech rondelles, Swarovski crystals: San Gabriel Bead Company

Seed beads: Jane's Fiber and Beads and Out on a Whim

Victorian Diamond Cuff p. 116

Freshwater rondelle pearls: TA Pearlstone and Evergreen Trading Company

Freshwater pearls: Lisa Kan Designs

Seed beads, charlottes, margaritas: San Gabriel Bead Company

Triple Spiral Garden Lariat p. 124

Freshwater pearls: Lisa Kan Designs

Seed beads, crystals, Czech fire-polish: San Gabriel Bead Company

Seed beads: Out on a Whim

SOURCES

Amulete Unlimited
8081 Sunflower Ave.
Alta Loma, CA 91701
www.amuletegems.com

Ancient Moon Beads
409 Mt. Auburn St.
Watertown, MA 02472
(617) 926-1887
www.ancientmoon.com

Anil Kumar
PO Box 3471
Fremont, CA 94539
(510) 498-8455

**A&P Trading/
House of Gems**
607 South Hill St.
Ste. #PL-02
Los Angeles, CA 90014
(877) GEMS-123
www.houseofgems.com

Bass Pro Shops
FireLine
(800) BASS-PRO
www.basspro.com

Bead Cache
3307 S. College Ave.
Unit #105
Ft. Collins, CO 80525
(970) 224-4322
www.beadcache.net

Beading in the Rain
(425) 895-1238
www.beadingintherain.com

California Collection
607 S. Hill St. #844
Los Angeles, CA 90014
(213) 489-1076

Evergreen Trading Company
607 S. Hill St. #431
Los Angeles, CA 90014
(213) 688-2723

Ezel Jewels
(814) 720-1806
www.ezeljewels.com

Garden of Beadin'
752 Redwood Dr.
Garberville, CA 95542
(707) 923-9120
www.gardenofbeadin.com

Gregory Benson
(508) 823-4951
EbayID: bogwondo

Jane's Fiber and Beads
5415 E. Andrew Johnson Hwy.
Afton, TN 37616
(888) 497-2665
www.janesfiberandbeads.com

JoAnn Fabrics
Sew on snaps

www.joann.com
Kelly Russell-Beadfuddled
(410) 609-0346
www.beadfuddled.com

Lisa Kan Designs
PO Box 80491
San Marino, CA 91118
lisakandesigns@yahoo.com
www.lisakan.com

Nina Designs
(wholesale only)
PO Box 2713
Emeryville, CA 94662
(800) 336-6462
www.ninadesigns.com

Out on a Whim
121 E. Cotati Ave.
Cotati, CA 94662
(707) 664-8343
www.whimbeads.com

Pearlbella Trading Company
22362 Homestead Rd.
Cupertino, CA 95014
(408) 737-0636
www.pearlbella.com

Rio Grande
Tools, beads, findings
(800) 545-6566
www.riogrande.com

San Gabriel Bead Company
325 E. Live Oak Ave.
Arcadia, CA 91006
(626) 447-7753
www.beadcompany.com

Soft Flex Company
PO Box 80
Sonoma, CA 95467
(707) 938-3539
www.softflexcompany.com

Specialty Beads
10280 Donner Pass Rd.
Truckee, CA 96161
(530) 582-4464
www.specialtybeads.com

TA Pearlstone
PO Box 22711
San Francisco, CA 94122
(415) 505-9148
www.tapearlstone.com

Vintaj Natural Brass Co.
(wholesale only)
PO Box 246
Galena, IL 61036
(815) 776-0481
www.vintaj.com

INDEX

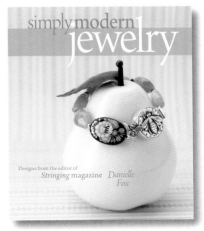